A Cup Story

John Mazzullo

First Edition

PAGE PUBLISHING, INC.
New York, NY

First originally published by Page Publishing, Inc. 2019

ISBN 978-1-64544-812-9 (Paperback)
ISBN 978-1-64544-813-6 (Digital)

Printed in the United States of America

Write what should not be forgotten.

—Isabel Allende

What you are about to read is true. The names have been coded to protect the unavoidable minor memory failings.

PERIOD 1

A Hill to Climb

In Madison Square Garden, no one can hear you scream. It was the Friday of Memorial Day weekend—the unofficial start of summer. The city had emptied as quickly as a ruck of insects from a dark basement at the flick of a light switch. But the boys of winter had a score to settle, a series to complete, and a quest for the world's most famous trophy to fulfill.

The NHL's Eastern Conference Finals between the New York Rangers and the New Jersey Devils had reached a seventh and deciding game. The Rangers were not only the top seed in the conference but held the (empty) Presidents' Trophy honor as the team with the highest regular-season point total (112). They were neither an army of lions led by a sheep, as Alexander the Great had once characterized opposing forces, nor an army of sheep led by a lion. The 1993–94 New York Ranger hockey club was an army of lions led by a lion.

The series with the Devils had been bipolar and forced the Rangers to the edge of elimination following a 4–1 defeat in game 5. Prior to game 6, to be played at the Brendan Byrne Arena, the *Panthera leo,* Mark Messier had proclaimed, "We're going to go in and win game 6."

Messier, with his guarantee, had not adopted the Ronald Regan philosophy that "When you can't make them see the light, make them feel the heat" but instead shifted the spotlight away from his team and unto himself. A three-goal response in a 4–2 victory had

Messier leading the pride back for a decisive game in their home arena in a city where—at that time of year—one could question if New York never slept only because most of its beds were unoccupied. The seats, however, at the world's most famous arena were most certainly filled on May 27, 1994, brimming, in fact, with hopeful anxiety.

The First Twenty

The crowd of 18,200 was clearly apprehensive throughout the scoreless first period. Prior to the renovation a few years earlier, the personality of the Garden was demonstrated through the primary seating colors—red, green, and blue and where some had argued conveyed a caste system. On that evening, the former red seats, where typically the affluent Wall Street crowd would fill, were littered with casuals and others who could not turn down offers from those regulars who were traveling for the holiday. And so the "Red Seats Suck" chants braying from the upper blues seemed hollow especially since teal had taken over. But the fans understood where they stood—and sat—even the novices. If you took in a Rangers game from the reds, you matched the personality of being an alpha, expecting the best that life offered.

The next level up from the lower bowl were the greens—loyal and frank fans that were self-aware and sensitive to their own reputation. The upper level—the blues—was the soul of the place. The faint cadence whistle would actuate from those rafters but what followed would stuff the building. "Potvin sucks." Those fans—the blues fans—were the most reliable and raucous, but even they, on that night, seemed skittish.

The Zelig was in the "old" reds that night with friend and colleague, Manno. They were offered seats from another friend Sean, a bond salesman from Kidder Peabody who had joined the Manhattan exile for the weekend. Manno and the Zelig were fans. They weren't pulling down the ticket offer just to attend an event. They were there to see the Rangers make another attempt at exorcising the ghosts of "nineteen forty."

The horn, signifying the end of the first twenty minutes of play, was as loud and startling as a ham-fisted road rager demanding that a daydreamer "Wake Up" and proceed through the green light. If the Devils strategy was to take the fans out of the game early, they were successful. No score, no penalties, and only a few decent scoring chances turned away skillfully by both team's keepers—Richter and Brodeur. If the Garden was an advantage for the Rangers, the reward for the Presidents' Trophy, it had been washy.

The narrow MSG concourses were bustling with agitated fans.

"What's Mess doing out there? His legs are shot."

"If I see another giveaway by Zubov…"

"I knew Kovalev would disappear in a big spot. You can't trust the Russians."

But the faithful were heard too.

"We got this."

"Richter's sharp."

The Second Twenty

The intensity was distinct at the start of the second period. The pace of play had quickened and the Garden faithful clamorous. The cutting sound of the skate blades slicing through the ice surface could no longer be heard. The thud of bodies battering the sideboards and the clacking of jostling sticks were faint. "Devils Suck" chants poured down from the blues like a torrent. But at the halfway point, the game remained scoreless. Until it wasn't.

At the ten-minute mark, the contest had, briefly, lost its shape and form. Players from both teams were out of position, the ice spacing disjointed, and the line changes jumbled. With the puck in the Devils zone, the big Rangers defenseman, Beukeboom, took the body to a Devil who iced the puck.

The ensuing face-off was won by Messier, and the puck found its way onto the stick of the sleek defenseman, Leetch, who sped behind the face-off circle toward the back of the net. Brodeur immediately closed off the short side with a tactical move to keep Leetch moving behind the net and toward his reinforcements. Leetch, however, had other designs. The defenseman's subsequent moves happened in a wink yet—from the Zelig's point of view—developed at a footpace. Leetch, a left-handed shooter, came to a sudden stop and yet, somehow, in the same motion whirled around to his backhand and thrust his body to that same short net side that that Brodeur had momentarily abandoned. The Russian Ranger—Kovalev—could (as it turned out) be trusted to come up big—darted into the crease directly in front of Brodeur just as Leetch arrived.

The details of how a puck slides past a goaltender and across the goal line—or at the back of the net—-were meaningless. What registers in that moment was the flash of the red goal light, the swell of a roaring crowd rising—in unison—to their feet, and ultimately the players thrusting their arms to the iconic roof at the Garden. Ranger goal.

All was right—for a moment—in the sporting world. The shared experience of celebrating the breakthrough was exhilarating. Awkward high fives that didn't land. Half hugs to nearby strangers and bellows of "Let's go, Rangers" put all fans on the same road map—the road to the Cup.

The second period ended with the 1–0 score shimmering from the scoreboard lights. The horde scrambled toward the concourse to celebrate the lead and share the mettle. A few brave Devils fans countered with talks of the "curse" and how the hockey gods would intercede and ultimately douse the crackling flame of optimism that bathed the square.

Why, after all, it had only been sixty-nine years earlier (sixty-nine as in, perhaps 1969, the year in which both the New York Mets and New York Jets relished in miracle championship runs) when—in 1925—the New York Americans became New York's first NHL team. The manager of the Americans, years later in 1936, was Mervyn Dutton. Red, as he became known, was a prototypical "red" seat personality—as life's ironies would have it—who left his Winnipeg college to enlist in "Princess Patricia's Light Infantry" and was subsequently injured as a World War 1 combatant. Despite his serious leg injury, Red turned to professional hockey in 1920. "I wasn't a good hockey player, but I was a good competitor."

With Madison Square Garden as the Americans first, and reluctant, landlord, the team turned an immediate profit.

Management acted logically and consistent with the tenets of capitalism where, to loosely connect to a quote by John Kenneth Galbraith, "Under capitalism, man exploits man."

And in the business of sports, those in false denial would claim, "It's just the opposite." So the landlord naturally formed their own team—the New York Rangers—which ignited a sports franchise war of sorts. Dutton, the Canadian serviceman, fought hard for the Americans. He arranged for financing to construct a new arena in Brooklyn. But the dream died following the death of then NHL president, Frank Calder. Dutton would go on to replace Calder, amid promises from the board of governors that the pursuit of professional NHL hockey in Brooklyn would be extended.

Ultimately and unfortunately for Dutton, the beats of the war drums were echoing once again. World War II had, among many of its other destructive wakes, killed the Americans (hockey team, that is) along with Red Dutton's vision. The legend would have it that Dutton declared vindictively, "The Rangers never will win the Cup again in my lifetime." He died in 1987, year 47 of the fifty-four-year "curse." "Nineteen forty."

The Third Twenty

Sociology professors have studied and written about the paradox of time—more specifically when time is perceived to be flying or crawling. One such study classified the paradox of crawling time into multiple categories including suffering, facing danger, boredom, high levels of concentration, and shock or novelty. The Zelig believes what the Rangers fans were experiencing throughout the third period was the shock or novelty that the Broadway Blueshirts were somehow actually going to advance to the Stanley Cup Finals. It clearly was not a reflection of the fan's high level of concentration—that was for the players to experience.

The Garden faithful had spent most of the early portions of the third period chattering and clapping—even shrieking—with no connection to what was happening on the ice. Perhaps they were concentrating on where to celebrate after the game. Despite the theories, time was dragging. Twenty minutes, after all, is twenty minutes from the standpoint of a scoreboard clock. The standard temporal unit is the same.

Every minute contains sixty seconds, doesn't it? But no, according to published conjecture. The "density of the human experience" where just the sheer volume of cognitive stimulation can lead to a sensory overload and create the sensation that sixty, godforsaken, seconds would appear to last from here to eternity.

Regardless of the crowd's psyche, the Rangers were pressing the action. "Do not sit on it!" The forwards were skating into the Devils zone and not just dumping and changing. Both teams exchanged scoring chances. Open ice checks, blade to blade passes, corner battles on display.

"Let's go, Rangers." The chant would ebb and surge and pull the entire fan base with it before momentarily flowing back into the darkness.

"Let's go, Rangers." It was back like a well-orchestrated symphony affording the brief silence to serve only as a launching point for the next wave.

The Rangers continued to have some control over the play when a stoppage occurred at—you are all paying close attention now and could have guessed—the one-minute mark. Sixty seconds for poetic license but factually seventy-one seconds for the historical record.

Spectators rose to their feet applauding as if just witnessing a Pavarotti aria. Bravo! Brave in Italian.

Or maybe to the end of the last of many Bruce Springsteen concert encores. "Bruce."

But, oh, those sixty, or so, seconds. Both Coaches Keenan and Lemaire used the stoppage to provide tactical instructions and implement the (final?) line change. As the home team, the Rangers possessed the last line change. The Devils had Nicolls, the face-off specialist, and Richer, a top goal scorer, with Lemieux, along with stalwart backliner captain Stevens and Daneyko.

One Devil player had not returned to the ice—Brodeur—pulled for the extra skates of Valeri Zelepukin. The Rangers countered with Beukeboom and Leetch as well Messier, Graves, and defensive minded, Larmer.

Face-off in the neutral zone. Nicolls won the draw, the Devils took possession and dumped the puck into the Ranger's zone. Clearing attempt failed. Scrum ensued. Graves with possession and was checked off the puck. He fell to the ice as the small mound of frozen rubber wobbled toward the sideboard. Messier was there and poked it forward just as Daneyko arrived. The puck tottered through the Devils zone and across the goal line. Whistle. Icing. Forty-eight seconds to melt away. Coach Keenan waved his arms in protest and to signal the referee McCreary. Messier skated alongside McCreary as they approached the bench. The Rangers argued that the puck was tipped by Daneyko. But McCreary was the sheriff, the lead dog. His job was to set the game direction and control the flow but not to flip-flop a call from the pleas of an unhappy coach. Keenan was not his musher. McCreary was barking at Messier and Beukeboom to assemble for the resulting face-off in the Ranger zone. There would be no appeal to the icing call.

Nicolls won another face-off. Messier collapsed awkwardly to his knees. "What's Mess doing out there? His legs are shot." The Zelig remembered the concourse gripes after the first period but would have none of it. No negative waves, Moriarty. The Zelig conjured up the *Kelly's Heroes* line from the actor Sutherland, "Why don't you knock it off with them negative waves? Why don't you dig how beautiful it is out here? Why don't you say something righteous and hopeful for a change?"

The puck ricocheted like a metal ball in an old arcade pinball game. The players chased with no plan in mind. Don't just skate there—do something! But nothing can get done on the shift. The formation was broken with the bodies strewed. Beukeboom gained control and zipped the puck out of the zone. Icing. No argument. Twenty-four seconds remained.

The *Kelly's Heroes* actor Sutherland had a son, another actor. Sutherland starred in a program *24* where the events were depicted in real time aided with a clock displayed on the screen:

Twenty-four ticks: Face off draw. The puck trickled toward skates of Leetch.

Twenty-one ticks: Leetch poked at the puck and deflected toward the end board.

Nineteen ticks: Beukeboom fired along the boards trying to clear.

Seventeen ticks: Devils pinched and maintained possession.

Fifteen ticks: Centering pass to Lemieux.

Fourteen ticks: Lemieux shot attempt right post. Richter pad save.

Eleven ticks: The puck slid across the crease past the diving Leetch and directly onto the stick of.

The Zelig and Manno and most other witnesses were being drawn to the combat as if directly involved. The Zelig could feel a stranger's fingers burrowing through the back of his neck as if kneading a plop of pizza dough. The Zelig was aware but did not care as he, too, reached for the hand of his buddy Manno as Thelma had to Louise before their fateful plunge. The Zelig thought he might have been shouting, screaming as he could feel his lungs roast a bit but could not hear nor did not care about the resulting sound.

Ten ticks: Zelepukin, the extra skater, whacked...nothing.

Nine ticks: Zelepukin jabbed.

A familiar refrain: The details of how a puck slides past a goaltender and across the goal line—or at the back of the net—are meaningless. What registers in that moment is the flash of the red goal light.

A different result. The Devils' Zelepukin scored. The first goal Richter had allowed in more than one hundred minutes of playoff hockey. Richter raced toward McCreary gesticulating with his arms to signal he had been interfered with. McCreary skated away. The energy level within the Garden had eerily remained kinetic. Missing was the deflated empty silence one would expect after such a dagger. Perhaps the Devils fans had been resurrected? Or maybe, thought the Zelig, the Ranger faithful had simply been victim to a beheading. Dare the thought but imagine the sight—headless chickens briefly running aimlessly before falling as lifeless clumps.

7.7 seconds frozen on the clock. Two sevens after a one (goal) had been rolled by the Rangers.

Craps!

The First Intermission

The Garden had become a cauldron of gloom. Not a word was spoken. The church bells all were broken. The restroom lines were tight and orderly. Silence, but for the sizzle of the giant "sweet tart" shaped urinal deodorants as the downtrodden fans did their business staring blankly at the wall in front of them. Mingling in the concourse after the conclusion of the third period was a torture. The concession lines appeared boundless with those waiting for the hottest selling item—brews. One man's misery is another's fortune. Perhaps the proprietors were pleased about the extended play. Nothing jacks up the beer sales like a steamy arena and a frantic fan base. But the Zelig had no stomach for it. Revisionist fans were moaning about how similar the game was to the first contest in the series where the Devils had rallied late from a one-goal deficit before winning 4–3 in double overtime. Maybe a quick lesson on conditional probability and independence would have been educational for the fans between their double-fisted swigs of dirty filtered tepid tap beer? Or, maybe not.

In the meantime, the Zelig's partner, Manno, had initiated a conversation with a couple of girls and rationalized those cues as a reason to return to the seats. The section was half-filled. The Zelig sat and glanced at the scoreboard. Eight minutes remained in the interval. The Zelig placed and clasped his hands behind his neck and relaxed for a moment as his mind sailed to memories of his past.

Seventeenth-century philosopher and physician, John Locke, believed that memory is the source of self-identity. Born in 1961 and raised in the Bronx, New York, the world to the Zelig appeared so expansive even when relegated to a few city blocks.

The homestead dwelling was a modest building with four apartments. In each of the apartments resided a member of the family. The grandmother and the uncle on the ground floor with another aunt and uncle across the corridor. A narrow stairwell led to two additional apartments where the Zelig lived with Mom and Dad and Sister and Brother with yet another Aunt and Uncle and Cousins unit "across the way." And a few miles away was another building with a similar familial structure (the relatives on the father's side). The Zelig's life was all family and centered around finding creative ways to "play." A common demand from the parents—"Go play." One activity was the discovery and use of a thin discarded futon mattress to rumble headfirst down the stairwell. At times, given a hard landing, the brother would blurt—"Bitch. Bastad." And when confronted by the downstairs aunt about the language and a threat of having the mouth washed out with soap, the brother would lower his head and bat the eyelids deferentially before whispering, "Bitch. Bastad."

The subsequent scampering escape back up the stairs was often more fun than the ride down. The roof was also a playground. It was accessible by an outdoor fire escape where the household children would often congregate and play. Once, when boredom won the idle mind contest, the mother's shoe collection was tossed off the roof into the alley below. The inevitable punishment of being hollered at or facing the threat of the father's belt would only be escalated by the brother's reaction. "Bitch. Bastad."

Sports was not a prevalent theme. Recreation was an occasional trip to the park where an hour "playing on the swings" felt more like a prisoner's legally required respite. But there was the Yankees—those Bums—as the Zelig recalled the father's description. A few times a season, the father would take the sons to the Stadium.

The pregame lunch packing ritual was the crescendo of excitement, and where who received the bologna sandwich on white over the salami and cheese Italian bread hero was the only real contest that mattered. The Zelig's memories of the Stadium were more about the sights and smells than anything that happened on the diamond. The father, sitting behind a field of view-obstructing pillar, would often nod off to sleep as the cheap cigar dangled from the corner of the mouth. The brother would take the opportunity to pluck a five-dollar bill from the father's trouser pocket and fuel a vendor splurge of Cracker Jacks, cotton candy, and cups of soda. The Zelig never recalled watching a game to its completion as the threat of traffic (or the father's conquest of beating it) dictated the departure time. On August 9, 1969, however, fandom—for the Zelig—was forged.

Old-Timers' Day at the Stadium. The father had been showing off his uncanny ability to name the Yankee "great" about to be introduced by the on-field host—Frank Messer—within seconds. "I can name that Yankee in two notes." The day was filled with pomp. Restored and freshly painted jalopies with waving players and happily strumming "Yankee-doodle-dandied" musicians circled the field. A packed stadium filled with more than fifty thousand adoring fans cheered endlessly as DiMaggio and Mantle were announced.

Were evolutionary biologists on point to explain this type of hero worship? Was it quite natural to look up to individuals who receive attention since they have attained a level of success in society? The eight-year-old Zelig could only process the moment in reverent wonderment and realize years later how the lasting memory helped mold his identity.

The Yankees organization had also provided the fans with a commemorative recording of Mickey Mantle Day that had occurred a few months earlier. The Zelig would play that vinyl countless times:

"Ladies and gentleman, a magnificent Yankee, the great number seven, Mickey Mantle." It was the voice of Mel Allen. The scratchy crowd roar lasted nearly ten minutes with no recess.

"When I walked into this stadium eighteen years ago," the Mantle recording echoed, "I felt much the same way I do right now. I don't have words to describe how I felt then or how I feel now, but I'll tell you one thing, baseball was real good to me, and playing eighteen years in Yankee Stadium is the best thing that could ever happen to a ballplayer."

The ovation was not for the words or even the sentiment, really. The continuous hurrahs were an expression of each fan's own personal memory. A true fan could associate a point in their life with what was happening at the time with Mantle and the Yankees, and so that part of the memory became just as important as the life event. An athlete can be admired for their ability and achievements, but the connection bred from athlete to fan was more about the impression of the residual experience and how strong of a building block the shared involvement was in the development of character.

Overtime

> You can observe a lot just by watching. (Yogi Berra)

Unlike the other major American sports, hockey is unique in that the game is not bound by structure consistent with baseball, football, or basketball.

Three outs per inning. Four downs per possession. Twenty-four second limit for a field goal attempt. That's not to proclaim it separates itself with an advantage but rather simply makes the game different.

In fact, it could be argued. The structure in the other sports creates tension and excitement, and where critics of hockey (and soccer to a similar degree) opine that the game's architecture could foster monotony. If the first overtime's game "action" was superimposed—for example—on a game played in November, the fans may have had reason to be bored. But there was too much at stake here for indifference. The players understood that there needed to be a differentiator in everything they were doing—even if it was to set up the next play, the next shift, the next period. The statistical outcome of the overtime period was a blank, but the Rangers were accomplishing something—if nothing else allowing their fans to grow confident again. The pace and style of play belonged to the home team.

Despite the lack of any real scoring chances, the Rangers were doing of all the "little" things. As the period wound to its conclusion, the energy in the building had been reignited. The scoreboard hadn't changed, but the spirit was back. The condition in the arena concourse following the overtime was a stark contrast to the end of regulation. The fans had discovered hope again, and the expressions of confidence were palpable. The Zelig, however, opted not to engage for the full break and returned to the seat alone where—once again—recollective thoughts prevailed.

Works of fiction need characters, but life has characters. In 1968, the Zelig and his family moved from the Bronx out to the "country."

The mother's sister had lived in what was described broadly by news media—following a 1978 murder-suicide within the school district's superintendent's office—as the "sleepy little summer hamlet of East Islip." Located on Long Island's south shore of Suffolk County, East Islip is where the Zelig was reborn.

The father, perhaps, had not been a huge fan of the move since his daily work commute to New York City via the Long Island Railroad had ballooned to nearly two hours in each direction. But for the children—now living across the street from their non-Bronx cousins—it was a renaissance. The modest ranch home was situated in a five-block parcel surrounded by a highway and an avenue blended among the neighboring houses and natural landscape as if intentionally camouflaged to appear not to appear. The Zelig quickly discovered the "fresh air fund" freedom of suburban life as he unearthed an appreciation for being surrounded by others his own age.

It would have been impossible not to immediately begin to develop—what would turn out to be—lifelong friendships and memories. On a typical summer day, the blocks would fill with eager children as quickly as a subway full of hurried commuters would spill onto a platform. There was no need to "call on" individual friends as a shared innate understanding existed on where and when to congregate. The Zelig, however, did have to adjust to the type of activities that were commonplace. He spent the first seven years of his life in the city. There was no need to own a baseball glove, a basketball, a hockey stick, a football.

But in suburban "EI," they were the necessities of life. Truly, the sole possession that aided in the assimilation was the cherished Mickey Mantle recording.

Where most of the other kids had baseball cards, the souvenir record was unique and became the Zelig's acceptance ante.

In retrospect, the games proved to serve as a vehicle to deliver some of life's key lessons, such as problem-solving, conflict resolution, communication behavior, and partnership success. And to think—all accomplished without an adult influence. The creativity that supported the games was impressive. The "EI" kids would conjure and enforce the rules depending upon where the games were played and the number of participants.

Certainly, there were arguments and name-calling and even an occasional scrap—but nothing that lasted longer than the time it would take for the dusk to dim the streets and for the inevitable Mom yowls commanding the children home for dinner. It was an "Etch-a-Sketch" world where each new day was a clean slate but also where the canvas was splashed with the color of the characters, such as TD, the ringleader, Sweet Lou, the free spirit, and Alan, the athlete. There were kids from the "other blocks" and kids that were just as much part of the fabric despite not participating in all the "reindeer games"—Andy, the blind boy, and Danny, the nonswimmer with the pool (above ground, of course). The array of personalities was a smorgasbord for the Zelig. The family (including the "surprise" addition of the younger sister) was ultimately immersed in the lifestyle. The kids didn't share the same "look," they didn't eat the same food nor did they talk the same way. The Zelig would be asked repeatedly to say any word ending in an "-er."

He complied for the laughs.

"Sweet Lou is a free swinga."

And they just loved the brother's "Bitch. Bastad."

Amid all the youthful fandom for the local teams, only two real rivalries were shaped—Mets versus Yankees and Rangers versus Islanders. While basketball was played within equal proportions and with just as much passion, the ABA's Nets were basically a punch line to the more established and successful Knicks. After all, who in the EI did not sport, or aspire to own, a pair of Puma Clydes? Eventually, the emergence of Dr. J sparked an interest in the other team that played at the Nassau Veterans Memorial Coliseum, but it never had the bite. The football equation was the most complex as it stood as a close second behind baseball as the most popular, on both a national and EI level. But the New York market was challenged due to the network television's "blackout rule." The Jets, at that time, played their home games at Shea Stadium, and the Giants performed at Yankee Stadium. Most often, the locals did not sell out the venues, and subsequently, the games would not be aired on local television. Therefore, on cold December Sundays, the airwaves were filled with Cowboys and Steelers and Raiders and Vikings. Additionally, the acclaimed weekly syndicated program produced by NFL Films, *This Week in Pro Football*, with hosts Summerall and Brookshier would mix audacious and brassy background music to the "Voice of God," Facenda's narration over three-quarter speed highlights. Who, ultimately could resist the image of the Packers as they ascended onto "The Frozen Tundra" or the sinful delight of the "Purple People Eaters?"

The Jets and the Giants, in comparison, were feckless and carried on faintly, obscured and inconsequential.

So the summer was dominated by Mets versus Yankees' debates. "Let's go position by position." And the winter was owned by Rangers versus Islanders when, mainly on Sunday evenings, TD would host Rangers' viewing parties in his basement and where the familiar voices of Gordon and the "Big Whistle" Chadwick would make you feel like you were at a family gathering and where the Zelig was first exposed to TD's buddies, Fisch, Prez, and Yrag. The cadence, energy, and language the Zelig experienced at that time was an exhilarating experience. Yrag, in fact, was Gary (phonetically backward). After a perceived cheap shot by Islander strongman, Gilles, Prez would bark,

"What a piece of 'tish' Gilles is." It was like pig Latin for those who never ate a slab of bacon or thought Latin was the language spoken in South America. The nights would also be filled with immediate impersonations of the Rangers announcing crew of Gordon and Chadwick:

"Knowing you, Bill, is like going to college."

"Fans throwing a beer can on the ice. Looks like a Schaefer, Bill."

"It can't be a Schaefer, Jim. Otherwise, there'd be more than one."

"Why give it to a guy with a pea shooter when you have a guy with a cannon right next to him?"

And while the mood would be predominately buoyant, the occasional outburst, "Tits!" following a negative play on the ice was met with a flick of the light switch and a rebuke from TD's mom to police the language. However, Fisch would always be positive. "No problem." The phrase was a creed and was consistent with the Fisch aura. A plasma ball of kinetic energy inside a stringy, spindly body. Fisch would extend an open palm high five regardless of the in-game plight. "No problem." Fisch also had credibility—to the Zelig—as his uncle Halligan was a connected public relations manager for the Rangers. "Uncle John."

Second Overtime

The puck dropped at center ice. Messier won the face-off. Rangers iced it. The Zelig's concern over the inauspicious start to the period was shared by others in the section as the remaining crowd filtered in from the concourse. Manno and the Zelig exchanged a jittery sideways glance hoping to telepathically wish away the ominous beginning. But the Rangers faithful took care of matters. A rousing "We Want the Cup" chant bloomed from the blues. Instant intensity.

The Rangers won the ensuing face-off and pressed the action. Keenan was not timid. The guns were out there. Messier. Graves. Kovalev. Leetch. Beukeboom. Let's go, boys. Skate! The Devils were having trouble escaping their own zone. On one such failed attempt, an obviously fresh-legged Matteau darted toward Brodeur on a play that had all the makings of a break-a-away but quickly foiled by a nifty Devils' poke check. Both clubs were showing fatigue.

The "free" ice seemed to expand as players struggled to close the gap on the puck handler. Long shots and quick line changes. Suddenly, a tsunami of red surged toward Richter. One. Two. Three Devils—in formation—skating with a purpose. One Ranger on defense. This is how it ends. The shot that kills you is the one you never see coming. A swell in the crowd. A whistle. Off-sides, Devils.

The professional athletes were exhausted both physically and mentally. This game will end by error, not by heroics. The Garden's air was stifling, and the ice was quaggy. The puck never seemed flat to the surface and was constantly on edge. Like the fans.

Beukeboom found himself alone at the blue line just inside the zone and directed a shot toward the cage. Blocked. A poor clearing attempt left the puck on Kovalev's stick. He wristed the puck through traffic at Brodeur. A gasp. Was the keeper beaten? Where's the red light? No goal. A left pad save. The rebound trickled away from the goalie as if a Ranger was pulling on a connected, invisible string. That Ranger? Messier. He was at the doorstep. He gathered patiently. The puck would not cooperate. It wiggled like a fresh catch on a dock. Messier managed to lift—aiming for the space under the armpit. Stoned. Whistle. Stoppage.

Messier's teammates surrounded him with encouragement as if he had failed rather than just bested on that play by the keeper. The building exhaled before play resumed. The action was sloppy. The referees also appeared weary and were caught out of position as forward Anderson was taken down without a called penalty and subsequently missed a retaliatory cross-check by the Rangers. The Devils were opportunistic and flashed an excellent scoring chance, but Richter coolly turned away a bullet by Richer. While only three minutes had elapsed, the sense that both teams were taking more risks was obvious. A trend emerged where the combatants had begun to tackle the anxiety of making a mistake head-on as opposed to playing it safe, hoping to avoid a costly miscue. Anderson, who had just been floored to the ice, was back for another shift and whistled a shot that Brodeur turned away. The Devils' MacLean lofted the puck skyward to clear the zone. Craned necks and widening eyes were apparent throughout the arena trying to track its flight. Perhaps the hockey gods above were roused. Another line change for both teams. Another distant Rangers' shot from the blue line soared high above Brodeur and clanked off the glass behind the goal. The puck bounded toward Rangers' forward, Tikkanen. He moved in quickly and unobstructed. The glistening of the ice caught the Zelig's eyes. "Where is everyone?" The rink appeared twice its size. Tikkanen could not do much with the puck and flicked it toward the opposite corner to Brodeur's right. Linemate Matteau had maintained his pep.

He was the first to arrive with Devils' defenseman Niedermayer in pursuit. Matteau raced around the back of the net just as Leetch had done earlier in the game for the lone Rangers' goal. Brodeur closed the gap quickly but—having been previously victimized by Leetch's "spin-o-rama"—he hesitated before sliding across the crease to his left. Niedermayer hooked Matteau to slow him down.

Two Devils charged the net like the cavalry. Defenseman Fetisov slid toward the left goal post as Matteau approached and center ice-man Dowd tangled with Tikkanen as he joined the fray. Matteau stopped skating and—from behind the net—extended his stick and stuffed the puck toward the corner of the goal mouth. The first sight to emerge from the goal crease was Tikkanen skating from the area with both arms raised. Matteau hopped gleefully like an innocent child experiencing hopscotch for the first time. Those sights were then accompanied by the roaring detonation inside the Garden. The fans looked to each other for confirmation. Goal? Goal!

The game winner. The series winner. Matteau had a double-overtime game-winning goal earlier in the series. And he did it again.

The fans were jumping, pumping exulting fists, and waving anything their sweaty palms could grip. One fan near the Zelig ripped the shirt off his back and waved it overhead as if trying to help a lost airliner find the runway.

Brodeur slumped dejectedly onto his backside inside the cage he had momentarily failed to protect. He rose to his feet slowly and pawed at the puck with his glove. The victorious Rangers were mobbing each other along the boards near the Devil bench.

"We want the Cup! We want the Cup!" The chant had replaced the classic "Let's Go, Rangers" incantation. A league official had rolled out the Prince of Wales trophy. Not a single Ranger went near it before Messier finally skated to the platform and lifted it impassively. The prize was not the prize. Only the chalice—Lord Stanley's Cup—would sate the masses.

The captain seemed aware he was hoisting fool's gold.

"We want the Cup! We want the Cup!"

The rhythmic hymn continued to consume the rink but whose memory would only eventually be muffled by what would become a New York Rangers hockey club psalm:

"Matteau! Matteau! Matteau! Stephane Matteau! And the Rangers have one more hill to climb, baby."

Yes, radio announcer Rose's iconic call had clearly defined the ensuing hurdle.

"But it's Mount Vancouver! The Rangers are headed to the finals!"

PERIOD 2

Mount Vancouver

Riot police fired tear gas, pepper spray, and flash bombs to try to disperse angry rioters who set cars on fire, looted stores, and taunted police officers. Police declared the area a riot zone and used batons and police dogs on the rioters. Police cars were set on fire in parking lots. Local hospital officials reported major traumas, stabbing victims, and head injuries. The mayor called the situation "despicable."

Such events, as described through news accounts from that certain city's officials, had never transpired in New York City following any major sporting event. But with both the New York Knicks and the Rangers in their respective sport's finals, the worst was anticipated. It could not be argued, however, that the city was not emitting a beacon of passion. Rangers' and Knicks' fans were, somehow, entangled in fruitless arguments about wanting to revel in the glory of an independent championship without having the spoils spoiled by having to share the spotlight with the other team. Nonsense. Let's be independent together.

New York was due for gluttonous sports pleasures especially since Major League Baseball, at the time, was attempting to foul off labor woes that were indicating a player strike was in the offing while the Yankees were leading their division.

But beyond those trivial headaches, the city was ultimately primed for a taste of good fortune. A year earlier, in February 1993, radical Egyptian religious leader, Sheik Omar Abdel Rahman, and a group of Islamic fundamentalists triggered an explosive left behind in a Ryder rental van parked in a World Trade Center garage. The blast opened a fifty-foot crater and caused the collapse of several floors. Six people were killed, and another thousand reported injuries.

Later that year, on a date—while linked in infamy—that was most likely just a sick coincidence, Colin Ferguson shot twenty-five passengers on the Long Island Railroad. Six of those December 7 commuters out of Penn Station never made it to their stop.

"Staten Island has the opportunity to participate in the creation of a city," declared John Marchi, a Republican state senator, following the approval of a city charter that laid the foundation for the borough of Staten Island to secede from the New York City.

Were these events symptomatic of the "Big Apple" rotting into a mealy, worm-infested settlement where the unruly would use a Rangers' or Knicks' championship to riot just as residents of the beautiful city of Vancouver had done in that despicable manner?

In August 1991, Crown Heights was the center of three days of violence between blacks and Jews that triggered disorder and unrest. Mayor Dinkins was criticized for not acting promptly to extinguish the clash and for his general lack of awareness. In the 1993 mayoral election, Dinkins' opponent, Giuliani, capitalized on the ineptitude and questioned the sitting mayor's competence, "It is patently clear that he can't manage a riot."

Giuliani defeated Dinkins and was the mayor in June of 1994. The city had experienced a renaissance of sorts.

New York's finest—the NYPD—appeared rejuvenated with the "carte blanche" the mayor had provided for them to take a more aggressive stance on crime. He was the "Nanny of New York," and the town had become a more civilized place. There would be no riots, at least not by the Rangers' fans design. But what of the Knicks, the other Madison Square Garden team?

"All of us have at least one great voice deep inside. People are products of their environment. A lucky few are born into situations in which positive messages abound. Others grow up hearing messages of fear and failure, which they must block out so the positive can be heard. But the positive and courageous voice will always emerge, somewhere, sometime, for all of us. Listen for it, and your breakthroughs will come."

Pat Riley, head coach of the New York Knicks, a Tony Robbins Svengali, had guided his tough-minded and strong defensive team to the NBA championship. With "His Airness," the GOAT, Jordan retired from the Bulls—who had defeated the Knicks the prior three playoff matchups—the Knicks were confident it was their time. But Jordan's sidekick, Pippen, was up to the task and led the team with "fiestas San Fermin" abandon throughout the hotly contested playoff series. Through six games—of which only one necessitated the scoreboard to utilize the all three available digits—the home team had been victorious. The Knicks prevailed in a slugfest, deciding game 87–77 by holding the Bulls to fourteen fourth-quarter points. Ewing, Oakley, Starks, Mason—the rugged core of the team represented New York so completely that the fans were hooked.

The Indiana Pacers, with its maestro—"The Garden's Greatest Villain"—Miller was the Knicks final obstacle to the finals. Unlike the Bulls series, this matchup between the country's basketball "mecca" versus "middle America" had the visiting team winning pivotal games 5 and 6 stretching the series to a game 7 at the Garden. Once again, the Knicks defense stymied the Pacers attack, holding the team to nineteen fourth-quarter points and winning 94–90. The Knicks were moving on to the NBA finals to face the Western Conference champion Houston Rockets.

The timing of Knicks' series, with the June 8 series opener in Houston occurring after the Rangers and Canucks had already battled for four games, had allowed for each team to own their own limelight. However, the exclusive notoriety each New York team feared the other would vanquish was stolen, instead, by a white Bronco.

"A modern tragedy and drama of Shakespearean proportion" was how the news anchor Brokaw described the "event" that others such as the sports anchor Costas had compared (as a shared cultural experience) to the Kennedy assassination or the moon landing.

Football legend Simpson and teammate Cowlings, who seemingly leisurely drive along the San Diego Freeway in Los Angeles, had filched the focus away from the hardwood and onto the roadways of West LA. NBC preempted its game broadcast to provide live feeds of the "chase" which culminated in the Juice's arrest on murder charges of the wife, Brown, and her friend, the waiter, Goldman. The network, years later, claimed there was a scant protest about the decision to hijack the hoops action but did provide split-screen coverage of game 5's conclusion which the Knicks won. In the end, and the truth be known (although not so much as to become a "spoiler" to this account), the June 17 Simpson shadow was not the only event that refracted the Knicks spotlight as, earlier in the day, more than one million fans had another reason to stretch across the "Canyon of Heroes."

Despite all the extraneous drama, the Knicks were traveling to Houston to complete the series they led three games to two.

Following a heartbreaking two-point loss in game 6, the Knicks would suffer from a crushing "picket fence" defeat in game 7 as the streaky shooting Starks only bucketed two of his eighteen field goal attempts for a .1111111111111 shooting percentage. If one is truly the loneliest number, Starks surely would have suffered in total isolation.

"All the critics and naysayers that looked hard at that and criticized the fact that John was still in the game, don't and did not take into account that we would have never gotten to game 7 if it wasn't for John." The master motivator, Riley, would not desert one of his own.

The hockey coach Keenan—in contrast to the basketball coach—portrayed his responsibility of becoming a championship architect as a plumber and not so much as Riley's dexterous phycologist. "We've got to build as a team and come together. We've got to be competitive every night and embrace the opportunity to deal with all aspects of the game. And right now, I feel good about where the team is at." Keenan, as expected, would need to employ all his tools to sustain the Rangers' momentum through what would become the clogged pipes of the 1994 Stanley Cup Finals.

The Rangers' roster had been transformed to match Keenan's style and philosophy. He built around players who possessed a mix of size, skill, and grit. To remodel, however, he needed the buy-in from the general manager Smith. A product of winning, Smith, who had worked for the Islanders during their 1980–83 four Cup run, was not fearful of reconstruction. The captain was brought aboard in 1991 on this general manager's watch:

"He had a huge influence on the franchise more than even on the team. He left a mark on the franchise that's going to be there forever. His presence changed the team from being perennial losers to almost perennial winners. "I wanted to end all that 1940 thing, the long-suffering and all that, and if anyone was able to be a silver bullet for all that, it was Mark."

Smith and Keenan were not deluded that the 1993–94 Rangers' roster was equipped for the Cup quest, and so changes were made. Top goal scorers Amonte and Gartner were moved for Keenan prototypes Matteau, Noonan, and Glenn Anderson.

The Gartner trade was difficult for the Zelig to digest since he had been a link to one of his more memorable Rangers experiences.

St. Patrick's Day began as a seventeenth-century religious feast tradition in observance of the patron saint of Ireland. The celebration broadened to include festivals and parades.

However, on St. Patrick's Day—March 17, 1990—the jubilee turned into a Nassau Veterans Memorial Coliseum melee.

The NHL scheduled the New York Islanders and the New York Rangers on a Saturday—St. Patrick's Day—afternoon where, perhaps not unlike the fate of Charles Dicken's character, Krook, in *Bleak House*, the fans spontaneously combusted.

The Zelig had joined a crew from EI on a bus trip to the game, and before the vehicle would have its gas tank filled, the real fuel was tapped and pouring freely inside. The usual suspects were all in attendance, TD, Sweet Lou, Prez, Yrag, but the scope of the trip and the enormity of the prospective partying brought out others, such as Joey D, Mito, the future state senator, the future Islander broadcaster, the lax goalie, George, and the brothers Albers.

The Islanders had introduced St. Patrick's Day beer sale specials hoping to bring the clientele and the revenue inside the venue. But management also offered an early, 9:00 a.m., parking for all ticket holders and tail-gaiters.

The EI bus arrived at the arena two hours prior to the scheduled 1:00 p.m. start time. The Coliseum parking lot was a prismatic sea of blue, orange, red, and white jerseys. There was also Celtic green sprinkled in. The tail-gaiting festivities were typical alcohol infused revelry with an occasional outburst of violence. The EI troop had two sets of seats in separate upper-tier sections.

As the crowd stumbled inside from the parking lot carousal, the Zelig anticipated the inevitable explosive union of flint and steel. The game's initial ebb and flow proved to be an accelerant for the ornery.

The Rangers struck early and lit the lamp first with less than four minutes into the period.

"Beat your wife, Potvin. Beat your wife!"

"Nineteen forty!"

Hot spots of fan turbulence erupted throughout the stadium. Security guards wearing bright-yellow jackets would swarm to the hornets' nest. The Islanders tied the game late in the first stanza.

"Rangers suck!"

Fans dived across aisles to join the latest breakout as the men in yellow responded to the wayward haymakers. There were three goals in the first five minutes of the second period—two by the home team sandwiched between a Rangers tally.

The air at the ice rink was hot, hot, hot, while the action in the crowd clearly eclipsed anything happening between the boards. The game officials occasionally halted play to allow the players to refocus and clear debris tossed from the seats.

Veteran Islander, Sutter, put the team ahead 4–2 as the second period concluded. The beer specials were discontinued. The security presence in the concourse was fortified. And the collective beer buzz was apparently wearing off until the start of the third period.

Mike Gartner put one past netminder Fitzpatrick to close the deficit to one goal. A member of the EI troop expressed satisfaction with the shift in game momentum. He rose to his feet and waved as a maestro would to communicate with his orchestra.

"Let's fucking go, Rangers!"

The Zelig witnessed an Islander fan rise and launch a cup of beer. Another fan followed, and soon it was raining men, hallelujah! Most of the conflict consisted of grabbing and tackling, but a few of the *forsai cosanta* felt some shock and awe was missing and ratcheted things up a bit. Within minutes, the entire section was brawling like an old Western saloon fight.

The brave men in yellow arrived to police the situation but the "brew-ha-ha" intensified. At its crescendo, the altercation turned ugly. The EI troop member had his adversary in a prone position and was about to chop some wood. A security guard arrived and grabbed the clenched fist from behind. The EI troop member whirled, and before he could disseminate who he was about to strike, struck. The security guard toppled and fell a few rows. The adversary had risen to his feet and jumped the EI fan from behind. They both bounced down the section and landed atop the security guard wedging his left shoulder between the seats.

Patrons from the neighboring sections raced toward the fallen and aggravated the situation. The security guard was blaring, trying to free himself. But the battle only increased until his comrades arrived in support. The EI fan, the initial adversary, and a mix of other pugilists were whisked away. The remaining security, with an assist from fans, freed the trapped guard who rose to his feet slowly holding his displaced wing against his chest for support. As the game continued, the EI crew followed the fan's escort to the concourse where they were greeted by a squad of Nassau County police.

The shouting claims of who started what and who did what to who fell to deaf ears. There was no time or place for justice. The cops were there to clean house.

The original two combatants were led by the police down a side stairwell. The future state senator calmly inquired where his EI brethren were being taken. The bus was going to the first precinct in Baldwin, New York.

For the time it required to assemble the EI troop to board the bus, the arrested fan could have easily been booked, processed, released on bail, tried, convicted, and time served. The coined phrase and comical task of "herding cats" would have made the exercise appear to be a US Navy Seal operation in comparison.

One EI crew member, George, arrived at the bus to find no driver, but the keys stowed under the visor. He proceeded to drive to one of the Coliseum gates. The driver, who had momentarily left the bus, pursued, apparently thinking the vehicle was being stolen.

Another EI associate attempted to reenter the Coliseum, apparently mistakenly believing the arrested was being held inside. He demanded entrance, stating he was the goalie for the New York Saints indoor lacrosse team. "It's not a lie—if you believe it."

Eventually, the EI bus troop reunited at the gate where the "stolen" bus had been waiting. Monetary bribes and profuse drunken apologies satisfied the driver who agreed to transport the bunch to the first precinct.

The prevailing, logical, reasonable thought would be that, given the recent events at the Coliseum, the EI party would be subdued on the trip to the "tank." But, with bloodshot "Irish Eyes A Smiling," one of the EI delegations tried to toss a quarter-keg of beer from a partially opened bus window. When confronted and questioned, the reply was simply "We killed it."

The bus arrived at the precinct where the future state senator informed the traveling asylum that he alone would handle the situation. No arguments from the peanut gallery as the onboard party was rekindled.

After approximately thirty minutes had elapsed, the future Islander broadcaster volunteered to obtain an update. When he didn't return, a suggestion surfaced to get the party bus heading back East and to a local bar to continue the road trip. No arguments from the peanut gallery. The future state senator, arrested, and future Islander broadcaster would be fine, reasoned some in that alternative universe. The driver complied and pulled away without a word. The trip home rarely even contemplated the plight of the EI members left behind but focused instead on the next stop of the caravan.

The St. Patrick's Day "massacre" ended sometime after 2:00 a.m. The prologue could be summed succinctly yet with a twist. The Rangers lost, and the Zelig was about to become a father.

The book *What to Expect When You're Expecting* provided a wealth of information for first-time parents, but none of which, however, delved into how the father can contribute and be supportive to the mother while massively hungover. Miracles do happen, and the Zelig and the wonderful wife gave birth to their first son on March 18, 1990.

The Series

The Rangers were awarded "home ice" in the 2-2-1-1-1 playoff format based on their league-best regular season point total which, in retrospect, did assign value to that Presidents' Trophy. The series opener, Tuesday, May 31, was the day after the Memorial Day holiday. The Zelig had not joined TD and Prez and another cohort, Volgende, in the shared season ticket Section 300 Green package since he often received ticket offers through his Wall Street connections.

The Zelig was counting on an availability of tickets for game 1 given its proximity to the summer holiday especially coming off the Friday "look" he and Manno had received for the Devils classic. But this was the Stanley Cup Finals—in New York City and with the New York Rangers. The Zelig's modest business dealings with the "street" couldn't even place him on the pecking order.

TD and his season-ticket group held a "draft" to allocate the games and he was designated games 2 and 7 (if necessary). The goal, however, was to try and attend every home game.

It was time to pull out all the stops which included the "Bifocal Bobby" scam and the "Uncle John" connection.

Bifocal Bobby was a Garden employee. He was stationed at the same gate for every game and would warmly greet the fans.

"Let's go, Rangers." His thick framed multifocal lenses would hang off the end of his nose seemingly ready to slide upon the Garden issued name tag "Bobby" that was pinned to his uniform just below the left clavicle. The good-natured (and vision-impaired) Bobby, however, had revealed a "tell."

When presented with a group of tickets, he would fan them briefly and do a quick guest headcount. He would straighten the batch of tickets and tear.

"Enjoy the game, gentleman."

The EI crew had begun taking chances to gain entrance into regular season games by combining unused preseason tickets with actual game tickets and targeting Bifocal Bobby.

The system had never failed. But was the fortitude there to try it for the Stanley Cup Finals?

One minimal downside risk was that Bobby would be moved from his typical gate. The other, more dramatic hazard, would be that Bobby would check each ticket's validity.

Act like it's a mistake was one rationalization or appear distraught and despondent that you grabbed the wrong tickets, and maybe Bobby will let you through with his typical ardor.

The rewards were worth the risk. The Bifocal Bobby scam was the plan for game 1.

Tibetan Buddhists utilize a technique to create a positive awareness by invoking sanguine images and associations. Once imagining a positive situation and achieving a feeling of optimistic emotions, it becomes difficult for the mind to also feel fear and anxiety.

The area surrounding Madison Square Garden before game 1 was replete with positivity.

The Vancouver Canucks finished second in the Pacific Division with 85 points (compared to the Rangers 112) and a 41-40-3 record. As the seventh seed, their playoff march was nearly sidetracked in the opening quarter-final round by the number 2 seed—Calgary Flames. The Canucks won the series opener, shutting out the Flames on the road, 5–0. But the Flames quickly regrouped and won the following three games to take a commanding three games to one lead.

The Canucks pushed the series back to Vancouver with a 2–1 game 5 victory. The next two—deciding games—were both won by the Canucks in overtime to win the series in seven games.

They breezed through both the conference semi and final rounds in five games.

This opponent was dangerous.

Piloted by experienced coach Quinn, the roster was fueled by the sixty-goal scoring, Russian Rocket, Bure, and the captain Linden. The netminder McLean was a two-time all-star and 1989 Vezina award winner, honoring the league's top goalie.

The Rangers and their thirsty fans were confident. There were no thoughts about getting this far only to lose to the Vancouver Canucks—of all teams.

The Zelig and TD were joined by Prez and Volgende, the actual ticket holders for game 1. The plan was for Prez to hand Bifocal Bobby the bundle of the two legitimate and two illegitimate preseason tickets and distract him with a line or two of the "Pig Latin."

The foursome arrived at gate C on the Thirty-third Street and Eighth Avenue coordinates.

Bobby was attending his customary station. His specs roosted on the bridge of his nose with the thick lenses clouded slightly from the humidity. The boys pushed through the channel of fans and positioned on bifocal's line. Prez separated the tickets marginally before handing to Bobby.

"Vig [Pig Latin translation—give] us a win tonight, right Bobby?"

Bobby reached for the tickets and gathered them quickly in his left hand. He pushed upward on the bridge of the bifocals toward the soft spot between his eyebrows.

"Here we go, Rangers. Here. We. Go!" TD boomed, pushing against Prez's back. A risky move.

RIP. The tickets were cleanly torn, and Bobby handed the stubs to Prez.

"See you, boys, Thursday night."

God bless you, Bifocal Bobby. The Zelig was in.

Experiencing the game action without a seat was manageable but not ideal. The Zelig and TD would alternate between visiting friends, briefly kneeling in the aisles inconspicuously and circling the outer concourse areas. The Bifocal Bobby plan was complete with a ticket exchange so that the actual holders, Prez and Volgende, would maintain the useless preseason stubs since they were posted safely in the rightful seats while the nomads held the actual ducats to be used upon potential inspection requests by suspicious ushers.

The Rangers christened the game action with authority if not discipline. Defenseman Wells was whistled for a cross-check within the period's first two minutes. The Canucks squandered the power play opportunity. However, the captain, Linden, was sanctioned for tripping.

Playing four aside, the Rangers were first to strike. Forward Larmer's shot from the slot beat the minder McLean on his glove side. The puck clinked the post and skidded against the back of McLean's skate before trickling across the goal line.

Taking an early one-goal lead in the first period of the first game stoked the hack prognosticator's claims of a "short series." The Rangers maintained pressure throughout the opening period as the Canucks were called for three consecutive minor penalties. The Rangers would not capitalize on the man advantage, and the score remained 1–0 after twenty.

The second twenty minutes belonged to the Canucks. The Rangers were sluggish to match the opponent's intensity and fell into the same careless, minor penalty trap that had befallen the Canucks earlier. But the goalie Richter stepped up and thwarted the enemy's power play. The Rangers gathered themselves for a late period push. McLean, however, was playing the part of Robert E. Lee's Confederate General "Stonewall" Jackson by closing the gaps against the Rangers attack. The Canucks appeared energized by the play of McLean as the game entered its final stretch.

In the mid-1860s, the budding printed press industry spun tales of the "Wild West" which fabricated and romanticized the actions of folk hero Jesse James. Against the backdrop of the Civil War, James and his gang's heists were compared to those of Robin Hood whose motivation was to rob from the rich and provide to the poor. The fact that James was also a notorious cold-blooded killer did not diminish the appeal of those fantasizing about the seemingly adventurous lifestyle. McClean's marauding performance in game 1 was juxtaposed with the swagger of the murderous frontiersman.

Early in the third period, McClean thwarted multiple scoring chances including a Messier breakaway and a subsequent puck clearing poke away from a pouncing Leetch. The Rangers continued to squeeze the Canucks, but their keeper remained buoyant.

Neuroscientific research on how individual brains focus is generally broken down into four categories. Focused attention, as defined, is the ability to focus exclusively on one channel or object of thought, regardless of the number of surrounding stimuli available to distract.

At the five-minute mark of the third period, the Canucks held puck possession in the Rangers zone when the referee thrust his right arm overhead without blowing his whistle, signaling a delayed penalty. The Rangers lost focus. Canucks forward, Adams, slid on his backside toward Richter with the puck just outside his stick blade. The Rangers were inert. Richter pushed the slow-moving puck away from his stacked pads as if he was reacting to a high-velocity slap shot. The rebound zipped directly to linemate Hedican. The unfocused Rangers remained stationary. Hedican slapped the puck between a sliding Richter's pads and into the net.

One. One.

The Ranger rebuttal, however, would not take long. Defenseman Leetch crossed the blue line with the puck. Three Canucks were drawn to him as if the Ranger great had a magnetic field surrounding him. Leetch continued to draw the opponents toward him as he drifted slightly toward the face-off circle to McLean's left. Kovalev, the Rangers' answer to Bure, sneaked into the zone and slapped the stick blade onto the ice. Leetch, without making eye contact, slid the puck directly onto Kovalev's stick.

Two. One. Rangers.

> We must build dikes of courage to hold back the flood of fear. (Dr. Martin Luther King Jr.)

Twice in seven playoff games, the Rangers had allowed their opponent to score a game-tying goal within the final minute of regulation. In the concluding seconds against these Canucks, the Rangers were showing signs of fear. The opponents were whirling around the Rangers zone establishing positions at key areas of the ice. The Rangers settled into a defensive cone extending from the front of Richter's goal crease out to the blue line. The tactics were fine. The intensity was missing. The Canucks were distributing the puck with ease across the zone but, like a cagey badger, were also slowly burrowing closer to Richter.

With just over that black magical one-minute mark remaining, a torpid pass from the undersized center Ronning wobbled lazily past a weak clearing attempt from the defenseman "Magician" Leetch who appeared as if under a spell.

Canucks forward Gelinas wristed a lollipop toward Richter. The puck was rising but was not traveling with velocity. Richter bounced faintly off his heels as his weight distributed to his toes. The puck was absorbed into the body, and Richter clenched to smother it.

Ronning skated in front of Richter appearing to stab at the air. Richter flinched briefly as the puck dipped between his left arm and knee.

Two. Two. Tied game. One minute on the clock. The third time in eight games that the Rangers had relinquished a one-goal lead in the final sixty seconds. A trend was born.

Overtime

> We don't see things as they are, we see them as we are. (Anais Nin)

Canucks goalie McLean continued his wizardry in the first overtime period. Scholars have described an optical illusion, in its most rudimentary form, as imagining the sun rising in the east and setting in the west. While the sun has not actually passed across the sky, the human eye and brain would interpret the image as movement.

As the Rangers swarmed the goal crease, in front of McLean, and fired point-blank shots at the net, the fans would stand and cheer in anticipation of what they had perceived to be the game winner. McClean alternated between a sturdy statue—repelling shots with limited body movement—and a contortionist—swooping from side to side and blocking shots with every available body part. On a few occasions, Rangers' skaters Graves and Tikkanen lifted their own arms triumphantly believing, incorrectly, the puck had traveled past McClean. Welcome to the grand illusion. Seventeen overtime shots on the Vancouver goal with not one resulting in one. The grand larceny had transpired for nineteen minutes of the twenty-minute session.

As the period moved into the final minute, the Rangers continued to dominate play. Tikkanen and Noonan were holding the puck behind McClean's goal, searching for an opening. The puck was cleared to the sideboard where a streaking Leetch received a pass. The ensuing shot was wide of the goal and caromed off the end board through the crease in front of McClean and traveled toward the opposite boards. Defensemen Beukeboom pinched, trying to keep the puck in the Rangers zone. The Russian Bure tipped the puck past Beukeboom against the board and maintained possession before quickly passing it ahead to Ronning.

With both Rangers' defensemen Leetch and Beukeboom having assumed an offensive role in the prior possession, only forward Tikkanen was in a position to defend as Ronning raced, undefended along the boards. Canucks forward Adams had filled the center ice area forcing Tikkanen to choose a man. Ronning keyed in on Tikkanen's movements, and at the instant, the Rangers' forward committed in his direction, he whipped a pass onto Adam's stick.

There would be no illusion in the next series of events. Richter "selling out" positioned six feet outside the crease to eliminate an angle with Adams winding his stick freely past his left hip and ripping the netting with the decider.

Three. Two. Canucks.

McClean skated quickly away from the goal mouth he had protected as if fleeing from a heist. His teammates joined, and they assembled in the Rangers' zone to celebrate the robbery. Rangers' color commentator for the Madison Square Garden network and fellow "Goalie Great" Davidson's observed:

"Canucks win this, it will be like Jesse James was in town."

Game 2

Uncle John was a longtime member of the Rangers' family.

"John Halligan was an institution with the Rangers and is much a part of the tradition and history as any player who has worn the sweater," said Glen Sather.

He was also married to Fisch's aunt Janet and so was also a member of the EI family.

Fisch was very respectful not to take advantage of Uncle John. In fact, the connection truly only broadened and deepened the devotion to the Rangers.

Occasionally, a "Rangers' fan club" perk would materialize including events at the team's training facility at Rye Playland and modest dinners where current players would attend.

Game tickets, while not completely out of reach, were not typically a benefit bestowed on Fisch. But that did not curtail the numerous friends' requests.

"No problem. Aunt Janet is a gem. Will see what Uncle John can do." The standard Fisch response very rarely resulted in tickets, but the upbeat way the message was delivered would often satisfy the requester. Fisch, on the contrary, took pride in his Rangers' autonomous monomania. He was transparent about the intermittent family benefits and tried to be inclusive but typically would conclude that self-reliance was way more fun. The optimistic spirit was a Fisch staple.

"If it didn't look good, I wouldn't be wearing it."

"I made the first move. I dare you to make the next." Fisch once included a headshot with a résumé submission along with a bullet point having a valid New York State driver's license.

"They need to know what I look like, and it shows initiative," he reasoned.

Fisch was clearly a strategic thinker, and occasionally, the tactical nature of life would escape him. At one point, Fisch was living at the home of the future Islander broadcaster when he fell asleep with a late-night snack nuked in the microwave. The subsequent small blaze and puny smoke billows aroused the entire household.

"No problem. Isn't that what we have smoke alarms for?"

Another incident involved Fisch, Sweet Lou, and the Zelig that involved Suffolk County's finest.

Fisch was driving home. The Zelig in the passenger seat and Sweet Lou in the rear plugging his earholes with his forefingers. An Aerosmith placard swung from its attached strings which circled the base of the rearview mirror. The mini marquee obstructed a segment of the windshield view.

"No problem." Fisch boosted the stereo volume.

The drummer, Bonham's kit pounding, and bassist, Jones, thumping felt as deeply as indigestion. The lead guitarist, Page, licking his "Les Paul" as if strapped with three of the twelve-stringed instruments. The singer, Plant, lip-smacking the harmonica before the classic chanting purr.

> Oh, nobody's fault but mine/Nobody's fault but mine
> Trying to save my soul tonight/Oh, it's nobody's fault but mine.

The divine Led Zeppelin cover of Blind Willie Johnson's 1920s blues vintage hit.

The approaching sirens and flashing patrol unit's lights were impossible to decipher, and so it was difficult to estimate how long they had been tailing the Fisch mobile. Sweet Lou's headrest battering sparked Fisch's attention, and he immediately pulled over without lowering the decibel level.

"Officer, it's nobody's fault but mine," Fisch replied upon the stern command to silence the tune and present the license, registration, and insurance card.

"Do you know how fast you were traveling?" the officer posed.

"No, sir. Isn't that what we have you for?"

Sweet Lou completed the drive home.

While Fisch was uniquely positive, he would not suffer fools gladly.

"There are no dicks on this bus," Fisch once barked in response to churlish behavior on a Massachusetts road trip where the EI crew was headed to participate in a "Mylec Dek Hockey" tournament.

"So before we leave, you better de-dick yourself."

Tragically, it was that feisty personality trait that ultimately determined Fisch's fate.

> There is no such thing as accident. It is fate misnamed. (Napoleon Bonaparte)

In the summer of 1988, Fisch had been assisting a DJ who often worked at clubs and parties in Manhattan. Following a gig that ended well into the morning, Fisch was alone and on foot. He was not the type to gauge the danger of a neighborhood and keep a low profile. Conversely, his friends believed, he had most likely been singing verses of Led Zeppelin or Aerosmith songs as he pounded the city pavement with his cherished "Frye boots."

"If it didn't look good, I wouldn't be wearing them."

The police report indicated the perpetrators who fatally shot Fisch that early summer morning had done so in a struggle for the boots.

"No problem."

The loss dampened the enthusiasm for the Rangers over the ensuing years, but the EI crew understood that no crime could be worse than allowing the light to be snuffed. Thereafter, the EI crew had not only rekindled the Rangers' spirit but did so in honor of Fisch.

Afterward, Uncle John would do his best to orchestrate game ticket connections upon request from the EI crew through Aunt Janet. A few of the boys had been hooked with games to the first-round sweep of the Islanders.

The Rangers "run" progressed through the Capitals, and Devils, tapping the uncle John connection seemed more impudent especially since his career path had changed from Rangers' public relations to working directly for the NHL's communications department.

Int. Stratton Oakmont III—Bull pen—day (Feb '95) Absolute bedlam. Three hundred drunken stockbrokers, most in their early twenties, chanted wildly as Jordan Belfort, handsome, thirty, stood beside a dwarf dressed in tights, cape, and helmet.

Jordan said, "Twenty-five grand to the first cock sucker to nail a bull's-eye! The 'bull's-eye' is a large dollar sign in the middle of a giant Velcro 'dartboard.' Watch and learn, people!"

The brokers went apeshit as Jordan grabbed the dwarf by his pants and collar. In the crowd, cash flew as side bets were made. Jordan winded up, aimed for the dartboard. One. Two. Throw! The brokers cheer, and as the screaming dwarf took flight, hurtling toward the camera, we freeze frame.

Working with Wall Street firms during the late 1980s and through the midnineties was not exactly the "strippers, dwarfs, and coke" world as depicted on the pages and film of the *Wolf of Wall Street.*

The Zelig worked on the "buy side" managing money for a large insurance company. His "street" connections consisted mainly of a hardworking fixed-income salesman whose main priority was to manage partnerships between the large investment banks and the institutional investor community. Occasionally, perks would be offered often in the form of steak dinners and sporting events.

For game 2 of the finals, TD had his green ticket from the draft. The "Bifocal Bobby" scam had already been used, and attempting the uncle John connection just seemed predatory. The Zelig happened upon the gracious generosity from one his sales coverage, known affectionally as the shark, the head of fixed income sales at a primary dealer.

At the pregame dinner, the conversation among the investment professionals was the probability of Canucks goalie McClean repeating his game 1 performance. The Securities Exchange Commission, after all, does require a disclaimer that "Past performance does not necessarily predict future results," and so that point was used as a topical argument designed to fulfill the prerequisite that business be discussed at client dinners.

The Zelig, however, voiced his concern over the troubling trend of the Rangers relinquishing one-goal leads within the final minute of play. A trend is "the general direction a variable is moving over time." And in nearly 40 percent of the most recent eight playoff games, the Rangers had succumbed to that trend. Notwithstanding the stark numbers, another theme would eventually emerge at the Garden on Thursday, June 2, 1994.

> I quickly realized that we were on unpaved ground, the plane started falling shortly after takeoff, and it was clear that we were going to crash. On impact, everything started flying. Something hit me hard. Once in the water, I honestly didn't see or notice anything around—not the fires, not the plane, nothing. (Alexander Sizov)

Sizov was among thirty-six hockey players and coaches, along with seven other crew members aboard a chartered RA-42434 tasked with transporting the Lokomotiv club from Yaroslavl, Russia, to Minsk.

The 4:00 p.m. flight on September 7, 2011, was scheduled for two hours and was intended to deliver the gods of Yaroslavl for their Kontinental Hockey League (KHL) season opener. What happened on that placid late summer afternoon was described by Brett

Popplewell as "the shortest journey and the darkest day in the history of hockey."

Two police officers had been on patrol in a river only a short distance from the runway. The ghastly sounds and images from the doomed, approximately—one-minute flight—propelled them to action.

"Brothers, help me!" It was winger Alexander Galimov. He waded through the wreckage strewed, shallow waters. He was on fire. "I can't see. My face, what's wrong with my face? What's wrong with my eyes?" He died five days later.

There was a church near the Volga river where the plane had crashed and exploded. A priest assumed a position at the location and rang the bell as the deceased were pulled from the water and remaining fuselage. One of those bells tolled for the Rangers' Alexander Karpovtsev.

On a historical perspective, the Black Aces were first commissioned in 1945 at a naval air station in Chincoteague, Virginia. Despite not being involved directly in enemy action, the Black Aces played a vital role in both World War II and the Korean conflict. Additionally, the Black Aces, in 1965, provided primary fighter escort for air strikes in North Vietnam.

Most notably, the group was the first squadron to utilize air-to-ground ordinances during "Operation Deliberate Force," a continuous air campaign carried out by NATO during the Bosnian War as well as support throughout "Operation Enduring Freedom" and its air strikes on the Taliban and al-Qaeda targets. The enduring spirit of the Black Aces is captured through "First to Fight, First to Strike."

The 1994 New York Rangers had their own Black Aces. The group had the reputation of being the first on the ice and the last to leave practice. The leader was Olczyk with other core members, Kypreos and Lidster and backup goalie Healy. Despite being a vocal and veteran group who knew that their respective roles were to energize the squad, "Heave ho! Pull together! Heave ho, pull together!" there was a more reserved comrade in the aces—Alexander Karpovtsev.

Raised in the Bronx, New York, John Amirante was a Rangers' fan from his pre–World War II youth. As he approached sixty-years of age, he kicked off each home game with a rousing rendition of the national anthem. At the start of game 2, the din of the Garden crowd appeared to take a few additional seconds before reaching its typically deafening decibel level. The Zelig wondered if the modest fan trepidation was caused by the Canucks' game 1 victory and McClean's achievement between the pipes. Was there a correlation?

Causation and correlation have been debated for years. American statistician W. Edwards Deming was once quoted, "In God we trust. Everyone else, bring data."

The data explains that causation indicates that one event is the result of the occurrence of the other event and correlation as a statistical measure that describes the relationship between two or more variables. A common example cited to assist with the causation versus correlation debate is that smoking is correlated with alcoholism but does not cause alcoholism. While smoking does cause an increase in the risk of developing lung cancer. So being behind in the best of seven series by losing the first home game is correlated to a somewhat sedated home crowd but would not necessarily cause a loss in game 2.

Following the Amirante anthem and puck drop, the Rangers played with immediate urgency. Two minutes into the period, the Canucks' Craven was whistled for tripping, and while the subsequent power play did not produce a Rangers' tally, the tone had been set.

Black Ace Lidster beat McClean soon thereafter, giving the Rangers a 1–0 lead, and he pointed toward the press area where his Black Aces' brothers watched—including Karpovtsev.

Lidster's goal revived the crowd and temporarily erased the McClean aura of invincibility.

The Rangers continued to dictate the tempo as the period neared conclusion. However, at approximately the fourteen-minute mark, it would become déjà vu all over again.

The Rangers attempted to assemble and break out of their own zone, but the Canucks were countering. A clean body check along the right sideboard displaced two Rangers from the puck. A shot from the blue line went astray to Richter's right. The pesky Vancouver skater

Conning captured the puck and skated to the left face-off circle just where he had been for game one's tying goal. Conning flipped a shot in Richter's direction as he moved to protect the left post. The keeper jounced and stiffened standing upright along the post.

The puck was not secure. It appeared motionless at the goal line as if placed carefully by hand. The Canucks winger Momesso was the first skater to appear, emerging from behind the net on the opposite side to shovel the puck home with his backhand for the tying goal. The momentum faded. The Rangers' radicals were awake to the fact that the team from British Columbia would not be easily conquered.

Located just eight miles east of Vancouver is Burnaby, British Columbia's third largest city and the home of Glenn Anderson, the son of Ann and Magnus and part of a generational commercial fishing family. Anderson's lack of appetite for the profession was evident at an early age.

"I was twelve on my first trip on the fishing boat. I was so sick I could never leave the bunkhouse. I could never go out on deck. I was hoping and praying we would get back to shore because I was so seasick that I couldn't stand it. But we got a mayday call and had to turn around and go back and look for a boat that went down. Planes were flying over, dropping flares. I made it out of a cubby hole, peeked over the rail, and went back."

Anderson's childhood apprehension had demonstrated an astute perception of risk as Canada's Transportation Safety Board's subsequent reports on the commercial fishing industry led to the proclamation of it being Canada's most dangerous job.

Nonetheless, Anderson had bestowed a vestige of good luck onto his hockey teammates by providing Mother Ann's salmon sandwiches as part of a pregame meal.

During Anderson's time with the five-time Stanley Cup winners Edmonton Oilers, another causation versus correlation example was conceived.

"Being superstitious, I don't want to talk about it," the captain Messier had once responded when questioned about the Oilers record following an Ann Anderson's salmon sandwich meal.

It was midway through period 2 when Messier assisted Anderson on a shorthanded goal to put the Rangers back on top 2–1. An empty-net goal by Leetch, inside the one-minute mark, pickled the victory and evened the series at a game apiece.

Game 3

> Don't give us none of your aggravation / We had it with your discipline
>
> Saturday night's alright for fighting / Get a little action in. (Elton John, "Saturday Night's Alright")

The Rangers and Canucks would meet in Vancouver on Saturday, June 4. Saturdays had not been kind to the Rangers in the 1993–94 season. The club's overall regular-season percentage of games won or tied was 71.5 percent, but they were a .500-hockey team on Saturday, including the only playoff loss to the Capitals and another to the Devils in the Eastern Conference Finals.

Thirty percent of all the Blueshirts' losses in the 1993–94 campaign occurred on a Saturday.

"Tony, the only way you gotta survive is to do what you think is right, not what they keep trying to jam you with. You let 'em do that, and you're gonna end up in nothing but misery," Frank Manero Jr. said to his brother Tony in *Saturday Night Fever*.

"Statistics are like bikinis. What they reveal is suggestive, but what they conceal is vital," said Aaron Levenstein. There was nothing to camouflage, however, as the Rocket, Bure, scored at the one-minute point of the first period to give the Canucks a 1–0 lead.

> Mr. Saturday night special / Got a barrel that's blue and cold / Ain't good for nothin'. (Lynyrd Skynyrd, "Saturday Night Special")

The Rangers did find a way to get hot as Brian Leetch and Glenn Anderson triggered the comeback with two late goals to put the team ahead 2–1.

With Leetch accounting for the lone second-period goal, the Rangers appeared to be gliding to a series lead. In as much as the squad appeared "loosey-goosey," there seemed to be something else at play on Vancouver's home ice—the Pacific Coliseum.

The ice surface at Madison Square Garden, especially in the late spring, was spongy and supposedly favored the veteran team. But the skaters from Broadway seemed to be flying at the "rink on the Renfrew." Their five-goal outburst in a March regular-season victory proved to be (in hindsight) a definite indicator of the team's affection for the surface. The steady—if not streaky—Larmer banged home the game's fourth goal just seconds into the third period and a game capping power-play score by Kovalev iced matters. The second time the Rangers scored five goals against the Canucks in their Hastings Park home and awarded them a 2–1 series lead.

> Saturday in the park / Can you dig it (yes I can) / And I've been waiting such a long time / For Saturday. (Chicago, "Saturday in the Park")

Game 4
The Save

The Rangers had peppered Canucks' keeper McClean with fifty-four shots in game 1, one for each year. The Rangers had ended their season without the Cup. He turned back fifty-two of them including seventeen in overtime to lead his team to victory and a momentum-building 1–0 series lead. The Canucks, however, had lost the edge and entered game 4 down 2–1.

Rangers netminder Richter, in contrast, was faced with one singular, decisive moment in the second period of game 4.

First period goals by Canucks' captain Linden and Rangers' bane Ronning had the Pacific Coliseum crowd delirious. Rangers' defenseman Leetch scored early in the second period to close the deficit 2–1. Two minutes following the goal by Leetch, it happened.

The Rangers were controlling play in their own zone. Forward Tikkanen found himself on McClean's doorstep, but his point-blank shot was deflected wide. McClean stood tall against a secondary shot from just inside the circle, and the puck trickled away from the goal mouth toward the center of the ice. Tikkanen was there again but quickly taken from the puck by two Canucks. Leetch snatched the abandoned rubber and moved deliberately from his left forehand to the backhand directly in front of McClean. His shot attempt was snuffed, and the puck spun toward the corner boards. Leetch pursued.

The resultant series of actions quickly transformed Leetch from the attacker to the prey as the puck drifted from his stick blade as if pulled by a strong undercurrent out of the zone.

The wunderkind Bure was there as if prepped and ready for launch.

> A rocket in its simplest form is a chamber enclosing a gas under pressure. A small opening at one end of the chamber allows the gas to escape and in doing so provides a thrust that propels the rocket in the opposite direction. (National Aeronautics and Space Administration)

Bure was gone. A streak of the Canucks' home white flashing across the ice.

Leetch and Beukeboom pursued. Leetch reached his stick and caught Bure's right leg.

He toppled. Whistle. Penalty.

The Shot

The referee Gregson provided Bure with instructions on the penalty shot as the Russian wiped his visor with a white towel.

"You cannot go backward, okay?"

Bure nodded in understanding as if there was any chance of that.

The Canucks' fans were cheering wildly, waving their own white towels. Richter patrolled his crease protecting the area as if they were his cubs. The whistle. Bure was in motion.

We have liftoff! Richter boldly skated quickly away from the net toward Bure ten feet from what he had cherished the most.

Brinksmanship is a foreign policy practice where parties involved force the interaction to the threshold of confrontation to gain an advantageous position.

President John F. Kennedy, in the fall of 1962, appeared on television to inform the American people of the discovery of a Russian nuclear missile installation in Cuba.

The crisis presented JFK with an option to order a surgical air strike against the bases in Cuba.

The military choice would have been provocative.

"If you are scared to go to the brink, you are lost," former US Secretary of State John Dulles said.

Kennedy chose a naval blockade of Cuba and warned the Russians that any missile attack from Cuba would be considered a Russian attack and would bring a "full retaliatory response" from the United States.

"The path we have chosen is full of hazards," the president relayed to the American people in a televised address. "But it is the one most consistent with our character and courage as a nation. The cost of freedom is always high, and Americans have always paid it. And one path we will never choose, and that is the path of surrender."

Pavel Bure immediately recognized Mike Richter's audacious maneuver and responded by thrusting speedily directly at the goalie. Richter began a slow, motionless retreat, drifting slowly back toward the goal staring directly into Bure's chest.

The brash act of brinkmanship had quickly reverted to a good ole game of chicken and not one unlike the famous James Dean bluff racing scene in *Rebel Without a Cause.*

The cars were in close, seen from the rear. Judy was a small distant figure. Arms stretched high.

The exhaust blasted. Now she dropped her arms. The cars leaped ahead. Judy whirled to see the cars snap by, then began running up the center of the plateau between the lines of spectators.

Cars approached, gaining speed, and thunder over the camera.

Inside Jim's car, he was tense.

Inside Buzz's car, his hands hard on the wheel. His comb between his teeth. He began edging toward the door on his left.

Bure approached Richter. The puck was positioned perfectly so that he could easily move both to the left on his forehand or to the right on his backhand. Richter was hunched into a compact ball. His limbs tensed but limbered enough to spring into action in either direction. He continued his deliberate pace backward toward the goal crease as Bure advanced.

Inside Jim's car, he edged to his left. He was driving with one hand. He opened the door, got set for his jump.

Inside Buzz's car, he reached for the door handle and missed. As he raised his arm to reach again, the strap of his windbreaker sleeve slip over the handle. He looked down in panic, then back at the drop ahead. He tugged but couldn't get the sleeve loose.

Inside Jim's car, his face was soaked. He looked once toward Buzz, then ahead. His eyes widened in fear. He shoved left and flung himself forward and out.

Inside Buzz's car, Buzz leaned way forward now. He seemed to rise in his seat. His mouth opened, and the comb fell out.

Rearview. Edge of the bluff as the two cars went over.

There was no human sound.

Bure twitched to his right hoping the move would cause Richter to believe he was going backhand and open a space to shoot at. Richter did not budge. Bure countered and charged toward the left goal post. There was no daylight between the players. Had Bure traveled too far?

Bure flicked his wrists abruptly trying to lift. Richter extended his legs and arms while maintaining a low center. Bure peeled away from Richter as a shark would after its first bite.

Richter bounced from his butt onto his skates as the puck emerged harmless directly in front of the arc of the crease. There was no goal. There was no crowd sound.

James Dean survived the game of chicken in rebel as Buzz remained in his car as it plunged from the bluff. Richter survived his encounter with Bure and put his signature on the series most memorable play. The goalie for the Rangers had done with one save what the keeper for the Canucks may have missed with his heroic game 1 performance.

A lioness and a vixen were talking together about their young, as mothers will, and saying how healthy and well-grown they were and what beautiful coats they had and how they were the image of their parents.

"My litter of cubs is a joy to see," said the Fox, and then she added, rather maliciously, "But I notice you never have more than one."

"No," said the lioness grimly, "but that one's a lion."

Quality, not quantity. (Aesop fable)

Three unanswered goals by the Rangers, including two power-play efforts by Zubov and Kovalev, provided the scoring margin in a 4–2 victory and a commanding 3–1 series lead.

The teams were headed back to New York City for game 5 and a chance for the Rangers to bring the Cup back to Big Apple.

Game 5
The Setup

In 1917, two young girls from Cottingley, England, took photographs of paper cutout fairies that one of the girls—Elsie Wright—copied from a children's book. Elsie and her ten-year-old friend, Frances Griffiths, innocently strolled down to a garden stream and posed with the spurious sprites. In the subsequent years, the innocent hoax gained traction and attention through the Theosophical Society, a group dedicated to exploring unexplained phenomena. However, with increased scrutiny, the photographs and the young girls were admonished as fakes and led many to ponder how a modest act of trickery can lead the masses to lose control of reality.

The scene at Madison Square Garden prior to the opening face-off of game 5 was a sham.

The Zelig was back with Manno, his colleague and counterpart from the Matteau game.

The tickets were provided by Jeff, an investment bank associate who was admittedly more of a fan of baseball and football. Jeff's firm had the reputation as a "Brother(s)hood," and the Zelig had participated in one of the better "street" extras they had sponsored and organized by the future New Jersey Devils owner.

The event was called the "Turkey Bowl" and consisted of the firm's employees, revered clients, and both current and former New York Giants football stars. The participants, including Andy, the Zelig's friend and work manager, would play in Giants' stadium with the game "action" recorded and later presented as a gift. Following the game, the fortunate representatives would dine in the Giants' dining lounge and watch *Monday Night Football.*

Jeff had agreed to host the hockey game if the Zelig didn't start any trouble as he had during a "Turkey Bowl" event where he (allegedly) paid a Fisch homage by asking that a former Giant wide receiver and fledgling politician who had been acting loutishly to de-dick himself.

It was instantaneously perspicuous to the Zelig and Manno that the Rangers' faithful had lost their minds as fans were pulling up on Thirty-third and Seventh Avenue in stretch limos, donning tuxedos, and sipping champagne. There were full-size Stanley Cup replicas on display. The crowd was howling, "Fuck you, nineteen forty." It was a group suffering from the euphoria of a perceived preconceived outcome. And they weren't alone in history.

November 2, 1948, Election Day, the Republican candidate, Thomas Dewey, a fearless, self-assured, mob-busting attorney and New York governor was poised to easily defeat his Democratic opponent and sitting president Harry Truman (assumed office in 1945 following the death of Franklin Roosevelt).

A weak economy and a fractured Democratic Party had created the illusion that Truman was doomed to defeat. However, the shroud of failure did not temper Truman's spirit as he campaigned across America. "Give 'em hell, Harry!"

In contrast, Dewey was busy counting chickens and ran an uninspired operation.

On Election Day, the *Chicago Tribune* was faced with a printer's strike which forced an early printing deadline. While the race had not been officially confirmed for either candidate, editors were so confident in a Dewey victory they went to press with the headline "Dewey Defeats Truman."

Manno nudged the Zelig as they entered the Garden on Thursday, June 9, 1994.

A fan held a *New York Post* high overhead. It was not the authentic copy with the headline "Tonight's the Night."

This counterfeit version read, "Rangers Win Cup."

A classic setup for the "confidence game."

"Andy Asshole. Andy Asshole."

The Zelig wondered if he was hearing the fans chant correctly. Andy van Hellemond was the referee for game 5. He had a checkered history with Rangers' coach Kennan.

In an interview, Kennan had explained how he had lost a three-goal lead in game 1 of the 1992 finals when his Blackhawks battled the Penguins.

"We were playing them well, and I felt that we could have beaten them. I was very disappointed in the league because of that series. It took us four years to get to that position, and now that we're there, look what happened. On Jagr's goal, not one, but two penalties could have been called against Pittsburgh on the play. Andy van Hellemond was the referee, and as far as I'm concerned, he's too veteran a referee to allow that to happen in the finals. There were penalties—holding of the stick was one—that could have been called against Mario Lemieux, but none were called. That tells me the league has an influence on who's ultimately going to win. It's a sad situation, but true, and it took the heart out of me and my team. We lost in four games, but it didn't have to be that way. It could have been different, and imagine the millions of dollars that were lost by the league because it ended in four. The league disappointed me."

"Andy Asshole. Andy Asshole."

Despite both clubs having quality scoring chances in the first period, the game was scoreless. The style of play was free-wheeling and reckless. Both goalies thwarted odd-man rushes and clear shots. But it was the Rangers who struck first.

Forward Tikkanen whistled a thirty-plus foot slap shot from just inside the blue line past McClean. The Rangers were rushing with numbers having a 3–2 player advantage when Tikkanen let fly. The crowd erupted. The goal light burned red. The chants consumed the arena.

"Let's go, Rangers!" Still something was off course. McClean did not show the emotion of a beaten keeper. He simply pointed with his glove hand.

The scoreboard remained at 0–0. And all hell had broken loose on the ice.

The Rangers' defensemen Beukeboom and Wells were scrapping with the pesky Canucks' Ronning and Momesso. The linesmen were shuffling from the scrums trying to restore order while the referee, van Hellemond, was monitoring. The crowd murmur continued to build as it became clear there had been a whistle somewhere and sometime before the Tikkanen goal.

"They called offsides."

As the officials restored control on the ice, the play was replayed on the scoreboard.

According to the boobird experts, the first written record of booing dated to ancient Greece at the festival of Dionysia in Athens. At the festival, Greeks would celebrate wildly in god worship, and plays would be performed. The crowd, often drunk from the wine that Dionysus (as the god of the grape harvest) had supposedly blessed the mortals with, would cheer and whistle in approval and boo and hiss disapprovingly at the work of tragedies.

"Booooo! Booooo!" While the play was close. The Rangers had entered the Canucks' zone legally. The goal should have counted. "Hello, insult. Meet, injury." The penalties were announced, and Beukeboom was cited as the instigator and levied with a fighting major and a game misconduct. The Rangers were down their best defenseman for the remainder of the game. The Canucks had a two-minute man advantage.

"Boooo! Andy Asshole!"

Somebody, please pass the wine.

The Con

The Rangers entered the third period in the preordained series decider—down one-zip on a second period Canucks goal by Brown.

The fans, although, were whistling past the graveyard. Confident and defiant, they were ready to complete the exorcism of nineteen forty.

Balboa knelt beside his wife, Adrian. Their newborn baby, Rocky Jr., swaddled and squirming between them. Rocky touched the infant's hand and told Adrian that he could find other ways to support the family instead of fighting the champion, Creed.

Adrian whispered for him to approach the hospital bed as the brother-in-law, Paulie, and trainer, Mickey, looked on.

"There's one thing I want you to do," she cooed. "Win...win."

The billowing of chiming bells, "Bong...bong!" induced chills. A rush of music. Rocky straightened and smiled.

"What are waiting for?" Mickey crackled. "Take this!"

The fans eructed at the scoreboard clip of Rocky II.

The puck was dropped at center ice. The Rangers' captain Messier watched from the penalty box, serving the remaining twenty seconds of his two-minute hooking minor from the end of the second period. The Rangers' Graves managed the face-off, and the Canucks gained control of the puck in their own zone and broke out quickly with the man advantage.

Vancouver entered the Rangers' zone effortlessly as the home team attempted to organize.

Defenseman Zubov aimed to clear the puck from the zone with a lazy flip from behind Richter along the right boards.

The Canucks' defenseman Hedican stopped the buck from escaping and lofted a shot in the general direction of the Rangers' goal. Vancouver forward LaFayette swatted at the airborne puck, and it struck Richter's pad. The goalscorer Courtnall was there for the rebound.

2–0, Visitors.

Red balloons floated toward the iconic ceiling. Were the Ringling Brothers still in town?

Fans in the Zelig's section were starting to spot the fugazies and snarling about those phonies dropping five grand to be a spectator of history and not really caring about the beloved Rangers.

"Let's go, Rangers!" Clap. Clap. Clap-clap-clap.

Uninspired.

The Russian Rocket, Bure, blistered a shot from the blue line. Richter stopped the puck cleanly. It crept away toward Leetch as he skated backward positioning himself between his keeper and an enemy forward. The puck kissed Leetch's right skate blade and redirected toward the open-goal mouth. Richter's slid on all fours as if praying for a miracle.

3–0, Canucks.

The Hoax

The Rangers' Russian Kovalev entered the offensive zone, skating with purpose along the boards adjacent to the team benches. The adversary from Vancouver, Glynn, smothered Kovalev's advance, and he put on the brakes. Black Ace defender Lidster had set up camp at the blue line, and Kovalev found him. Forward Larmer arranged himself in front of both the minder McClean and defenseman Lumme. Lidster cast the puck airily toward the net traffic.

Larmer stabbed his stick as the puck waft toward McClean. McClean's attempt at snaring the puck was that of a butterfly catcher. However, his catching glove was not a net, and the puck floated directly into the top corner of Vancouver's.

> Butterflies are free to fly / Fly away, high away, bye bye. (Elton John, "Someone Saved My Life Tonight")

3–1, Canucks.

> The journey of a thousand miles begins with one step. (Lao Tzu)

The Rangers were back in the game.

Play resumed, and the action was nonstop. No whistles. No icing. No pucks in the crowd. Fluid, hard-checking, in-your-face hockey.

"It's my last game, and I wanna play it straight," said Paul Newman as Reggie Dunlop in *Slap Shot*. "I wanna win that championship tonight. Old-time hockey, like when I got started, you know? Eddie Shore...those guys were the greats."

The Hanson brothers replied, "Yeah, sure. Old-time hockey! Like Eddie Shore—yeah! Coach, our line starts?"

The Rangers started with their line of Larmer, Matteau, and Nemchinov.

Nemchinov won a loose puck battle behind the Canucks' net. Larmer reinforced and kept the puck breathing along the boards. Nemchinov relieved and gained control as Larmer and Matteau crashed the goal. The defenseman Zubov entered the fray and darted in front of McClean. Matteau tangoed with a Canuck inside the crease to McClean's left.

Nemchinov shot on the goal. McClean fell onto his back as the boxer Sonny Liston had done from the phantom punch by the great Ali in Maine circa 1965. The puck presented itself to Larmer who snapped it into the goal. A brief dispute about Matteau's crease presence but clear that the tango dance required two to complete. Goal stands.

3–2, Canucks.

The Garden crowd, like the team they were fanatical about, had found the stride. The buzz in the arena had morphed into a steady rumbling roar. There was no need for artificial chants or manufactured enthusiasm. This was Rangers' hockey. Old-time hockey.

The players on both teams were selling out on each possession. The checks had a purpose. Each inch of the ice was contested. Holding. Grabbing. Clutching. "Andy Asshole" had swallowed the whistle.

The Rangers were amid a beleaguered line change when the Rocket, Bure, went into orbit. He controlled the puck in the neutral zone and, following a few rapid strides, sent a torpedo at Richter, who had abandoned his crease to eliminate an open angle. The puck caromed from his pads and the captain Messier gathered the rebound. He deftly left the puck for the defenseman Lowe and continued skating from the zone behind the net and along the right boards. Lowe advanced the puck quickly, and in a blink, the Rangers had assembled an attacking formation. The forward Anderson was streaking at center ice and received the puck. Canucks' keeper McClean had adopted Richter's strategy and attempted to eliminate a shooting lane. Anderson, however, shrewdly slipped the puck between his legs in a blind back pass to Messier, who had continued the trek from his own zone along the right boards.

McClean was forced to adjust and overcompensated with a decisive move to his left.

The captain, wittily utilizing a Canucks' defenseman to partially obscure his intentions, guided the puck at the area of the goal just outside McClean's right blocker and goal stick.

Ranger goal!

Knotted at three.

The suddenly United Nation fan base—consisting of both the die-hard and Johnny-come-lately fannies—were off them. A sustained standing ovation for the team that, in a span of six minutes, had restored the faith and provided a reason to believe again.

The Zelig and Manno were extolling the virtues of playoff hockey—championship hockey—to their host, Jeff. He was standing and cheering. A spontaneous apostle.

The enduring salvo would not relent, and the coming face-off was slowed. The Zelig's thoughts flitted to reconciling the concept that he could be on the cusp to bear witness to history—to a New York Rangers' Stanley Cup championship. The Zelig ruminated on his ability to remain composed, if it were to happen or, rather if he would be overtaken by the mournful retrospection that was lurking in his mind.

> Martin Sloan, age thirty-six, vice president in charge of media, successful in most things but not in the one effort that all men try at some time in their lives, is trying to go home again. And also, like all men perhaps, there'll be an occasion, maybe a summer night sometime, when he'll look up from what he's doing and listen to the distant music of a calliope and hear the voices and the laughter of the people and places of his past. And perhaps, across his mind, there'll flit a little errant wish that a man might not have to become old, never outgrow the parks and the merry-go-rounds of his youth. And he'll smile then, too, because he'll know it is just an errant wish, some wisp of memory not too important really, some laughing ghosts that cross a man's mind that are a part of the Twilight Zone. (*Walking Distance, The Twilight Zone*)

The memories of Alan, from the Zelig's enshrined EI childhood, were never as abstract as some sort of reminiscent specter. Alan, still, remained as much a part of the Zelig as his other lifelong companions, TD and Sweet Lou.

Alan was the gifted athlete of the EI gang. His baseball skills, especially, were extraordinary and unmistakably innate. The natural abilities fueled the enthusiasm. The variations of play were innumerable and ranged from whiffle ball to innovative games using the Spalding "hi-bounce."

Additionally, the EI boys would invent other modified baseball-centric activities.

Inventions of "dice baseball" where fictional leagues were formed and where games were played with the resulting dice roll corresponding to the outcome of an at bat.

Two was a triple. Three and ten were doubles. Seven was a single. Eleven was a walk. Twelve was a homer. Four, five, six, eight, nine were all outs. Statistics were maintained in a myriad of loose-leaf notebooks. Later, the boys were introduced to more advanced games such as Strat-O-Matic.

Indeed, the amount of time spent on these activities was more a pretext to the gratification of simply having spent the time together. Hours would pass watching an 8mm film of the Ali/Frazier *Fight of the Century* at Madison Square Garden and listening to the vinyl of the *1969 Miracle Mets*. The Zelig and Alan were also *The Twilight Zone* aficionados and created a log of the episodes. But the headline act was always baseball.

The Little League of the Islips was a slice of suburban baseball with well-manicured fields located within walking distance of the Zelig's neighborhood.

The Zelig and the EI crew called those fields their own. During periods of inactivity, when the fields were scheduled for maintenance, the EI crew would sneak on to play. Sliding on the dewy, freshly cut outfield grass, fielding grounders on the packed clay infield, and lacing up the cleats on the benches of a concrete dugout would be worth the risk of getting caught and chased from the diamond by the head grounds crew supervisor, Sonny.

"Is this heaven?"

"No, it's East Islip,"

The Zelig, a Yankee and Roy White fan, played his little league for the hated Mets. But the sour taste of playing for the enemy was sweetened by the initiation and subsequent solidification of another lifelong friendship with teammate Joey I. (or Joe EI).

Alan, a Yankee and Thurman Munson fan, was an Indian.

TD, a Mets and Tom Seaver fan, was a Tiger.

But Sweet Lou, a devoted Lou Pinella fan, relished the serendipity of being a Yankee.

> Worship is transcendent wonder; wonder for which there is now no limit or measure; that is worship. (Thomas Carlyle)

The origins of Sweet Lou's kindred connection to Lou Piniella is murky. Perhaps he was enamored with Piniella's clutch performance or his savvy on the diamond. But the affinity was so authentic that Sweet Lou mutated to an excitable boy at the chance to meet his idol.

December 1978, East Islip High School sponsored a fund-raising event, and Lou Piniella was scheduled to appear to play basketball. Sweet Lou would not be unprepared to fraternize with the Yankee great. However, a combination of nerves and alcohol botched the following checklist:

- Customized Sweet Lou T-shirt—ordered adult large and received youth large.
- Yankees cap—misplaced. A replica Yankees batting helmet was the replacement.
- Pre-event cocktail to calm the nerves—shots of vodka to obliterate the faculties.

Following the successful event, Sweet Lou and Piniella posed for a photo. The debate raged for years whether it was the ill-fitting clothing, apparent protective headgear, slurred yet animated whooping—or all the above that explained Piniella's belief that Sweet Lou was the 'special' honoree of the charity affair.

During its peak, late spring evenings at the major field, where the twelve-year-old boys would play, the scene was straight out of a Norman Rockwell. The aroma of hot dogs and soft baked pretzels would emanate from the concession stands. The spectator chatter would be broken, momentarily, by the public address volunteer announcing the approaching batter. While the landscape was not exclusive to that "sleepy little summer town" on Long Island's south shore, it felt that way to the boys of East Islip.

The Little League of the Islips directors understood the colossal popularity of baseball during that period—when the tail end of the baby boomer generation drove the demographics—and extended little league to players past the cutoff age of twelve. Senior league allowed the boys to continue to play on regulation size fields with sixty-foot six-inch mound distance and ninety-foot bases. The two main fields used for the senior league were on the grounds of the East Islip High School. And it was there, in the late spring of 1975, where heaven had mutated to hell.

The high school complex was also within walking distance from the Zelig's neighborhood, but the trip involved crossing a highway and a parkway. The area around the school fields was isolated with a two-lane spur connecting an elementary school with both the high school and junior high buildings. Practice times on Saturdays were typically staggered between 9:00 a.m., 11:00 a.m., and 1:00 p.m. The Zelig had the 9:00 a.m. slot on that direful Saturday morning. Alan practiced at 11:00 a.m.

The Zelig would love to have remembered a lasting exchange or a final moment together that could have been a memory adhesive. But, sadly, there was only the recollection of the teams exchanging places on the field, and the Zelig (most likely driven by hunger) was in a rush to head home.

A few yards of brush separated the spur and the parkway. The Zelig scurried through the wooded area and emerged at the ridge of the roadway. A glance left then right before hustling across the grassy median separating the east and westbound lanes. A clear pathway and another dash to a grassland leading up the highway. The Saturday morning traffic was (most logically) light, and so the Zelig had an accessible jaunt across the four lanes of traffic separated by a scant metal divide that could be hurdled without effort. The Zelig began a light jog through the blocks of his community toward his home.

The father was happy to bring the son back to the ball fields to retrieve the baseball cleats the Zelig had left behind after quickly changing into his sneakers before leaving the field. Approaching a traffic light that controlled the flow of cars from a boulevard to the spur, the father was redirected by a police officer. The disconcerting warning sirens filled the air as police cars turned onto the spur. The father pulled off the road adjacent to the scene, and the Zelig headed on foot toward the school.

Earlier, as the Zelig hiked home from the fields, Alan had sprung from his "on-deck circle" position to retrieve a teammate's batting practice foul ball that had cleared the fence surrounding the field and landed in the scarce thickets that divided the spur from the parkway. He retrieved the ball and hustled back to the field. As he approached the fence and readied to scale it, Alan dropped the ball, and it rolled back onto the spur. It was then, at that single innocent moment of fetching a baseball, when Alan was struck.

The Zelig's arrival to the scene was after Alan had been placed in the ambulance. Those present were somber, crying, and traumatized. The Zelig heard a comment about the illegality of transporting a dead person in an ambulance. Another witness said the last words Alan spoke was "It hurts" as he gasped for breath, broken on the spur.

Hours later, a reporter from *Newsday*, the Long Island journal, called and spoke to the Zelig.

Through tears of confusion, fear, and distress, the Zelig's quote to the young female reporter capped her story of Alan's tragic fatal accident:

"It's hard to believe something like this could happen. One minute, he's there, and the next, he's gone."

The successive days when the Zelig cleaned out Alan's school locker and the dutiful funeral home attendance was a stupefying fog. In fact, the one element that persisted was the memory of Elton John's recently released hit "Someone Saved My Life Tonight" (also previously cited in this account) that the EI crew listened to in those dark days of mourning.

"Butterflies are free to fly / Fly away, high away, bye bye."

The crisp October air did very little to alter the flight of the toilet paper rolls that were streaming onto the outfield grass of Yankee Stadium.

Perhaps the impassioned fans were venting, having watched a nemesis. The Royals' third baseman Brett continued to punish the Yanks by blasting a three-run, eight-inning home run into the same right-field seats where the tissue paper was spilling. Brett's blast tied the fifth and deciding game of the 1976 American League Championship series at six apiece.

The grounds crew completed their cleanup, and Yankees' first baseman Chambliss was motioned to enter the batter's box. The Royals' relief pitcher Littell had been pacing and blowing moisture into his cold hands throughout the delay. He toed the rubber quickly upon the umpire's instructions and delivered a fastball to Chambliss.

The Zelig could never explain the bewildering and abrupt rush of emotions that conquered him as he watched Royals' outfielder McRea leap for the Chambliss bid to place the Yankees into the World Series for the first time since 1964 when they lost to the Cardinals and ceased to be the Yankees.

As McRea slumped to the warning track disgusted over his empty glove, Chambliss toured the bases by mowing through the horde of on-field spectators as football great Brown had done throughout his dominating NFL career.

Watching the starved Yankee fans swarm the field as ants onto a discarded watermelon rind, the Zelig cried. The tears were unexplained but spilling down the cheeks nonetheless.

It wasn't until the father joined in the celebration and asked why the Zelig was crying that the enigmatic emotions were accepted.

"Alan."

"A Mask hid his Sensitivity."

The Zelig sobbed as he pedaled his bicycle home from the nearby delicatessen on August 3, 1979. He held an edition of *Newsday* that printed that headline to describe the Yankees' captain Munson and detail the events of his demise practicing takeoff and landings in his newly purchased Cessna Citation aircraft at Akron-Canton Airport on the prior day.

Thurman was Alan's favorite Yankee.

The Sting

Do human behavior drive actions of those that—when feeling overly confident—will take risk and become careless? Sigmund Freud believed that the criminal mind, in its unconscious state, displayed a desire to get caught from an overriding sense of guilt.

The Rangers won the face-off following the captain's game-tying goal and immediately surged into the reeling Canucks' zone. The Zelig was surprised to find himself seated as play on the ice resumed. A poke from Manno, "Let's go! We're winning this," or something to that effect snapped the Zelig from his reverie. The Rangers' Kovalev, Matteau, and Larmer were each along the far boards, opposite the player's bench and to McClean's right. They were winning the puck battles briefly but were in no position to take advantage of possession. They didn't seem to know where they were going, but they were on their way. The defensemen Leetch and Lowe were shrinking the Canucks' zone and positioned inside the blue line. But speed kills.

The Rocket, Bure, managed to absorb the puck along the boards where all three of the militant Rangers' linemates were trapped. He rushed along the boards out from the zone as Leetch attempted to use the barrier to keep the Russian from controlling center ice.

Bure zoomed to his left and outpaced Leetch. The Canucks had the numbers. Three skaters to two defensemen. Bure was in complete control. Neither Leetch nor Lowe could commit to try and check him from the puck, and so they back-skated trying to minimize the open lanes available to attack Richter.

The Canucks' veteran defenseman Babych was the opportunistic recipient of the perfectly timed and placed pass from Bure. His shot easily beat Richter, who had been slow to react to the least obvious threat the Canucks had presented.

Thirty seconds from the euphoric Stanley Cup dreams had ticked off into a one-goal mole hole.

4–3, Vancouver.

The Rangers' play and the Rangers' fans sharpened immediately following the goal. Perhaps a flock of the pretenders had flown from the Garden when the Blueshirts fell behind. The fans were on every play. A billow of excitement as the Ranger' Nemchinov received a nifty pass and startled McClean with a brisk snap of the wrist. The goalie's pads were just squeezed enough, however, to prevent the knot goal. Hoots and cheers would accompany smart checks and crisp play, and the stage appeared to be set for positivity. When Messier suddenly appeared at McClean's doorstep, the crowd thundered in anticipation. The keeper denied the captain's offering. As the Canucks' defenseman Lumme skated cleanly and untouched from his own zone into Rangers' territory, the fans snorted in fear. Lumme found his compatriot, LaFayette, who responded with a thumping shot into Richter. The goalie's save produced a healthy rebound, and the winger Courtnall blasted the puck behind a sprawling Richter for a 5–3 lead.

The two-goal deficit had felt like a gopher hole.

The hopes of a Cup celebration were just a feint. Or were they? Was there time for an epic comeback? Did this team have the fortitude to take it home? The fans felt victim of a con job. Research shows that the first step in handling a fraud attack is "Do not blame yourself and put the blame where it belongs—on the people who conned you."

But were the fans to blame? Had the baseless certainty that the Cup would be secured on that night stemmed from the team or from themselves?

> The fault, dear Brutus, is not in our stars, but in ourselves. (Shakespeare)

A Rangers' shot was tipped and spiraled into the crowd.

A face-off was conducted outside the Canucks' zone which Vancouver won. The defenseman Hedican traveled unaccompanied through center ice as both Bure and Ronning bracketed.

Another odd-man rush. The Rangers were clearly no longer careless or aggressive or reckless. The team had flat out quit. Hedican pass to Ronning. Ronning shot on goal. Rebound to Bure. Score. 6–3 Canucks. The hole had become a crater. The marks were hustled.

> You have to keep this con even after you take his money. He can't know you took him. (Henry Gondorff, *The Sting*)

With seven minutes reaming in game 5, the Rangers continued to skate and pass and shoot and check. But the jig was up. The announcement of Bure's sixteenth playoff goal echoed through the arena. An air-horn pierced the hushed Garden as a drunkard tooting a noisemaker. Hours after the midnight celebration had passed.

The organist attempted a reveille. Wake up!

Goodnight, Nurse.

Game 6

> In space, no one can hear you scream.

A *Planet Earth* series on BBC not only describes a black hole phenomenon but also speculates and describes what would happen if someone would fall into one.

"The instant you entered the black hole, reality would split in two. In one, you would be instantly incinerated, and in the other, you would plunge into the black hole utterly unharmed."

The Rangers were headed west to Vancouver, British Columbia, to clash with the Canucks for a sixth game on another Saturday night, no less, after missing an opportunity to capture the Cup in game 5 in front of their deprived fans.

"A black hole is a place where the laws of physics break down. The gravitational field is so strong that not even light can escape, rendering the region to be profoundly dark."

The Canucks fans greeted the Rangers with rousing chants."Nineteen forty! Nineteen forty!"

"We want the Cup! We want the Cup!"

Vancouver emerged from their space tunnel flying. The Rocket, Bure, sent the tone with a ballistic hit on the defenseman Leetch.

One of the Canucks sixteen first period shots eluded the keeper Richter, and Vancouver—holding the Rangers to only seven shots—lead 1–0 heading into the second-period horizon.

"As you accelerate toward the event horizon (the point at which the gravitational force counteracts the light's efforts to escape), you stretch and contort and appear to move in slow motion."

The Canucks continued to skate circles around the Rangers in the second period. At the twelve-minute mark, forward Courtnall levied a big bang into the apex of Richter's body movement and where the ascending node of the puck across the goal line was boosted by the defenseman Lidster's stick.

"You sail straight into nature's most ominous destination without so much as a bump or a jiggle. You are in freefall, something Einstein called his 'happiest thought.'"

The referee McCreary whistled the Canucks' center McIntyre for too severe a form of propulsion into the goalie Richter. The Rangers' center Kovalev took advantage of the power play and released a g-force shot where the puck's nadir was in the direction of center iceman Craven's skate. Occultation occurred as the puck found a safe passage between the pads of McClean to cut the Rangers' deficit in half, 2–1.

"You reach the horizon and freeze like someone has hit the pause button. You remained plastered there, motionless, stretched across the surface of the horizon as a growing heat begins to engulf you. You are slowly obliterated by the stretching of space and the stopping of time. Before you ever cross over into the black hole's darkness, you are reduced to ash."

The Canucks' defenseman Brown scored his second goal of the game midway through the third period to stretch the lead to 3–1. With time running low, Vancouver's Courtnall appeared to have secured his own second goal of the game, but the officials made no motion, and the play continued. The Rangers' Anderson beat McClean just seconds following Courtnall's apparent score. The game was ostensibly a 3–2 thriller with less than two minutes remaining.

However, upon review, Courtnall did—in fact—score, and so the Anderson goal was negated, and the contest's final ballistics were irrevocable.

4–1, Canucks.

Series tied at three games each.

The deciding match was to be played on Tuesday, June 14, at Madison Square Garden.

PERIOD 3

This One Will Last a Lifetime

Game. Seven. The two most exciting words in sports.

"Overture, curtains, lights / This is it, the night of nights / This is it, you'll hit the heights /

And oh, what heights we'll hit / On with the show this is it."

It was as if Bugs Bunny himself was present at the Garden for the game 5 con job. But the Rangers and the fans would have had to learn their lesson. Game 7 would not be about the bogus grandeur. It would be about the play.

The Ranger players had adopted diverse attitudes about the challenge. Veteran Ranger MacTavish, for example, and the comedian, short fictional character, Nathan Thurm, assumed a similar approach.

Mike Wallace (character) said, "Pardon me for saying this, but you seem defensive."

Nathan Thurm (*Saturday Night Live* character) replied, "I'm not being defensive! You're the one who's being defensive! Why is it always the other person who's being defensive? Have you ever asked yourself that? Why don't you ask yourself that?"

MacTavish, who had experienced the Cup reign with Messier's Edmonton Oilers, when questioned about the Rangers fearing that their championship was slipping away after suffering two consecutive losses, responded with the following:

"Game 7 of the Stanley Cup final has a calming effect," he explained. "You've got to count your blessings and go from there. It is hockey in its simplest terms. You win one game. You win the Stanley Cup. Do you have to put a negative spin on it?"

Another seasoned Ranger, Tikkanen, who had also contributed to the Oilers Cup dynasty, presented a different perspective.

"This is it. There is no other way to approach it. This is our last chance to win the Cup!"

Tikkanen's enmity was a familiar tone for Rangers' fans as it was akin to one of the many crowds prompts the club would utilize at the Garden home games; the famous Peter Finch clip from the film *Network*:

"So I want you to get up now. I want all of you to get up out of your chairs. I want you to get up right now and go to the window. Open it, and stick your head out and yell, 'I'm mad as hell, and I'm not gonna take this anymore!'"

Despite the psychology of the moment, it had arrived. But earlier on that warm June 14 afternoon, the Zelig had come to terms to where he would be viewing the spectacle—home.

The Zelig had spent the workday trying to snag tickets by pulling on any available strings, cashing in on any free spin chips and just simply laying on the sympathy.

However, the perks cupboard was bare. The Zelig reasoned, in the end, that it would be gratifying to watch the game at home.

The wonderful wife had been a tremendous sport over the preceding two months, allowing the Zelig to live vicariously through his New York sports heroes. Additionally, rationalized the Zelig, how fruitful the shared experience would be with both of his sons, as the family had welcomed the second child in 1992. Plus, the Zelig persisted to delude himself. It would be more responsible to be away from the expected chaos that would follow if the Rangers were to win. It was time to grow up and become the accountable adult and the mature father. And he had whiffed on tickets.

Manno had also tried futilely to secure tickets. He informed the Zelig that he too had abandoned the hunt and planned to take the game in at an Upper East Side bar.

The Zelig was about to call home and let the wonderful wife know he would be coming home for the game. The phone rang. It was TD. Was he calling to gloat since he had already been locked in with a ticket from the green seat lottery?

"I'm out, TD. No tickets. I couldn't work anything."

The Zelig was instantly skeptical of TD's resulting proposition.

"The what now?"

It was an offer from Mike O., an EI associate that the Zelig knew moderately from TD.

He was the eldest in the O family with brother Kevin and sisters Christine and Kelly who were more contemporaries with the Zelig than the older Mike. The O family patriarch was a New York City Police Department luminary.

TD explained to the Zelig that the brother, Kevin O., would be attending the game with the assist of an NHL press pass that the patriarch O. had obtained and allotted to his son, Mike O.

"We have two extra," TD expounded. "You in?"

The wonderful wife would understand and explain to the two toddler sons that Daddy would not be coming home that night.

The Zelig could not reach Manno in time, so he made a few calls and walked the floor to offer participation in the arrangement. Most of the colleagues were dubious or busy or indifferent. There was one exception, Mark, the intern, had not hesitated, responding with an emphatic, "Shit yeah!"

"Gulliver lies down on the grass to rest, and soon he falls asleep. When he wakes up, he finds that his arms, legs, and long hair have been tied to the ground with pieces of thread. He can only look up, and the bright sun prevents him from seeing anything. He feels something move across his leg and over his chest. He looks down and sees, to his surprise, a six-inch-tall human carrying a bow and arrow. At least forty more little people climb onto his body.

"Gulliver struggles to get loose and finally succeeds in breaking the strings binding his left arm. He loosens the ropes tying his hair so he can turn to the left. In response, the little people fire a volley of arrows into his hand and violently attack his body and face. Gulliver is tempted to pick up forty or fifty of the little people and throw them against the ground. He is struck by their bravery since they climb onto his body despite his great size."

When the New York Yankees star pitcher Gomez publicly wondered why the 1941 team would replace the legendary infielder Crosetti with the Lilliputian. He would have no idea that Rizzuto would, one day, become a Yankee giant and hall-of-fame celebrity.

The Scooter had lived with the comparison to those characters in *Gulliver's Travels* throughout his career. In 1949, when the fabled skipper Stengel assumed the Yankees managerial role, the categorically established Rizzuto was described as testing his skipper.

"Mister Stengel, sir," he deadpanned, "do you think I'm too small to become a major leaguer?"

New York Times' reporter Daley asserted that "Casey chased him right out the door with a baseball bat."

The Zelig had invited Mark, the intern, to a Yankee game earlier that year in a suite hosted by a major investment bank. The Yankee Stadium "luxury boxes" were known for their modesty. While the affair was spirited with generous helpings of good cheer and ballpark grub, it lacked the accouterments of other street largess. That was until, of course, he graced the suite with his presence.

The Scooter. He was amiable and gracious. He told a few stories and shook a few hands. He thanked the patrons for supporting the Yankees. And he posed for a group photo.

The Zelig had positioned himself perfectly off Rizzuto's left shoulder as if a pirate's trusted parrot. Mark, the intern, flashed his pearly whites joyfully posing next to the legend.

“Enjoy the game, you Huckleberry’s!” Rizzuto departed.

The mood in the suite was spontaneously animated, and the humble surroundings had magically transformed into an ornate palace.

“Your mission, should you choose to accept it, is to place the NHL press pass lanyard around the neck and keep it visible at all times. You will follow Kevin into the Garden, but once inside, you must separate. Avoid sustained eye contact with Garden employees. You will meet at the green seats after the game. As always, should you be caught, we will disavow any knowledge of your actions. This offer will self-destruct in ten seconds. Are you in?”

The brother, Kevin, read Mike O’s mock *Mission Impossible* directions from an index card.

TD had joined Kevin at the Eighth Avenue rendezvous.

“Oh, they’re in,” he woofed presumptuously.

The Zelig and Mark, the intern, nodded affirmatively as Kevin O. placed the golden tickets around their necks. The foursome approached a side entrance on Thirty-fourth Street between Seventh and Eighth Avenue.

“See you guys in there! Good luck.” TD was off to his own legitimate entry point.

His departure placed a modicum of trepidation into the Zelig’s chest.

> Walk into the place like we own the joint. (The character Barney, *The Pope of Greenwich Village*)

He and Mark, the intern, followed Kevin O. through the vestibule. The Zelig reached for the lanyard for display to the security guard. Kevin O. nodded. "No." He walked ahead. "Watch me."

The security guards obviously detected the NHL press passes and allowed entrance into Garden tacitly.

"Don't go around flashing this," Kevin O. motioned to the pass. "You should act like you don't even know it's on you. These guys know what to look for."

Message received.

"See you boys at TD's seats after the game." Kevin O. was gone.

Mark, the intern, informed the Zelig that he was going to the suite of the same investment bank that hosted the Rizzuto outing. He had apparently kindled a relationship with a young female employee of the firm. It was great to observe that the kid was learning something.

The Zelig was on his own. Furnished with the carte blanche press pass, he followed a small gathering to a rickety elevator and entered. The group scattered instantly as the doors opened, and the Zelig walked slowly to the area where the anthem singer Amirante was positioned. It became clear, at that decisive moment, that the experience for the Zelig was going to provide an entirely unique perspective.

Inspecting the crowd from that vantage point created a sense of detachment. The Zelig felt like an observer instead of a participant. Amirante walked onto the ice from the staging area. The Garden was black. A spotlight on the ice marked the spot for the singer. The Zelig inched closer to the tunnel's mouth. The Canadian anthem began, and the fans chanted.

The powerful singer was overpowered by the chanting. The display appeared disrespectful.

Suddenly, however, the chanting ceased, and Amirante could be heard. It was as if by intuition, the fans simultaneously understood the inappropriateness of the actions.

They began to sing along.

"O Canada, we stand on guard for thee."

There was no segue, and no possible way to foretell what was about to transpire. The evidence that Amirante was singing the "Star Spangled Banner" was irrefutable. But not one simple note nor lyric could be heard.

The sustained, deafening barrage of cheering never even assumed a rhythmical pattern. It sounded as if the clamor was piped into the arena on a digitally recorded loop. The Zelig's head tingled, and while not remotely wired in a narcissistic manner, he almost felt as if the adulation was directed at himself. The sheer energy of the moment tugged the Zelig closer to the ice surface where he could see a fan holding a sign from a sliver of brightness emanating from the floodlight.

"There is a God."

Colossians 3:17 said, "And whatever you do, whether in word or deed, do it all in the name of the Lord Jesus, giving thanks to God the Father through him."

While even the most devout do not actually believe that God cares who wins or loses sporting events, there is an acceptance that God can use anybody in any position to bring Glory to His name.

July 12, 1986, a twenty-nine-year-old New York City police officer was patrolling Central Park. During a routine questioning of three youths about a recent rash of bicycle robberies, one of the young men pulled a weapon and fired three bullets. The damage from one of the rounds shattered the officer's spine and rendered him paralyzed from the neck down.

Later that year, at the baptism of his son, the officer's wife, Patti, spoke to a group, huddled outside the chapel, to inform them of her husband's desire to make public that he forgave the boy who shot him.

Officer Steven McDonald said, "Once you let go of the wrongs that have been done to you, it changes everything. I could have gone the other way. I could have been overcome with emotion, bitterness, and anger. Patti called them wasted emotions. I could have killed myself. I tried to. God always found me, and with the help of others, I got through it all."

The Amirante anthem ended. The lights were on. A whir continued to infuse the Garden.

The Zelig noticed a woman approaching. She was assessing him. The Zelig looked down. His hands were touching the handles of a wheelchair. Seated in that chair was Steven McDonald.

The Zelig calmly retreated as the woman advanced. He deliberated momentarily whether the guidepost moment was symbolic of some deeper spiritual sensitivity, or had the result of his scam just coincidentally landed him next to the revered officer. The Zelig was not about to linger to figure it out. He was on the move.

The Zelig was leery of invoking the "Bifocal Bobby" routine of encircling the outer concourses to take in the game. So the first planned station stop was to visit Sean, the salesman who had provided the Devils' game 7 tickets. Alternating between observing the "on ice action" and gauging the crowd's temperament, the trip to Sean took most of the first period.

The signs that players on both teams were nervous was pronounced. The combination of skill and physicality needed to play the sport is quite unlike any other. The first ten minutes of the activity was void of skill. When in doubt, hit someone! There appeared to be ten checks for every shot on goal for each team throughout the early portion of the contest.

During one brief stop on the Sean pilgrimage, the Zelig heard fans talking about how important it was for the Rangers to strike first so that they could play from ahead with the lead. Unable to resist, and feeling legitimized with his NHL press pass, the Zelig countered with thoughts on the recent troubling trend of the Rangers' squandering late leads.

The lack of satisfaction from these exchanges did not surprise the Zelig. The fans were not there for debate. They were there for a great awakening.

A broad smile and a warm embrace greeted the Zelig as he faced Sean. Before any conversation could occur, they were alerted to promising on-ice developments. The sleek defenseman Leetch received a precise pass from his blueliner mate Zubov. The image of the Vancouver goal mouth appeared cockeyed. There was nobody home. The keeper McClean was well out of the crease, and there were two Canucks and one Ranger in the vicinity blocking the goalie's view. Leetch calmly deposited the puck into the vacant area. And the fans had been given their early lead.

Rangers, 1; Canucks, 0.

The Zelig and Sean chatted briefly, but the commotion inside the arena made it challenging to continue. They agreed to meet up at some point after the game. The Zelig was then called away by a group of young men who worked in his Manhattan office building.

It turned out that there were other gumptious Rangers fanatics who had devised methods to get into the games without tickets.

This bunch was electricians from (one of) the local union shops. They informed the Zelig that the union cards and corresponding work uniform had been sufficient to gain entrance into a handful of games throughout the year—including the playoffs. They were somewhat circumspect about rolling out the plan for game 7. Their fears were unfounded.

The Zelig was reticent in explaining the NHL press pass dangling from his neck and provided a few vague details before changing the subject to a fellow colleague and friend of both groups, the honorable Mr. Lee. As that conversation petered, the Zelig was ready to bid the electricians adieu when a rumble of thunder crackled throughout the Garden.

The Rangers' forward Anderson was slumped along the ice in front of the Rangers' bench. Blood trickled from a gash on his nose apparently opened by a wayward Canuck stick.

Despite the vocal protests, there was no penalty called on the play. As play resumed, the motivated Rangers had dominated the action.

As if a cat toying with an inanimate ball of string or, perhaps more appropriately, teasing a prone prey, the Rangers would not allow the Canucks to escape their own zone. The Rangers maintained possession for nearly a full minute before a Vancouver defenseman Lumme was called for cross-checking the Rangers' unhelmeted one, MacTavish. The coach Kennan pounced. He placed his top line and power play unit—Messier, Graves, and Kovalev on the ice immediately.

The Canucks managed a clearing, and Richter strayed far from his goal to play the puck and reduce the time needed for Vancouver to get their penalty kill unit in force.

The Rocket, Bure, forechecked effectively to provide the time that Richter was trying to lessen. The cat and mouse game was won by the Rangers. Zubov, while checked from the puck just before entering the Canucks' zone, managed a pass to Kovalev who promptly found a streaking Graves who sailed the puck behind a prone McClean.

The chosen led 2–0 after one period.

> A heart at peace gives life to the body, but envy
> rots the bones. (Proverb 14:30)

The Zelig was feeling oddly isolated from the conspicuous hysteria consuming the Garden at the first intermission. He reasoned that his feelings were caused by the unorthodox way he was involved in the conceivable historic event. He wasn't at game 7 as a true fan but an imposter. As he walked the bustling concourses, the Zelig battled thoughts of jealousy to those he witnessed reveling in the unaccomplished.

> 'Cause when you worry your face will frown /
> And that will bring everybody down
> So, don't worry, be happy. (Bobby McFerrin,
> "Don't Worry Be Happy")

The Zelig had planned not to go to the green seats with TD until the third period, and so he made his way to the suite where Mark, the intern, was being entertained. The luxury box was raging. Mark, the intern, was feeling no pain. The party was on! The Zelig chatted it up with a few members of the hosting firm, and the conversation centered mostly on the hockey.

Someone yelled out a statistic about the Rangers being 8–1 after leading following the first period. The finding paled to others by comparison, for example:

"Perhaps today was the most exciting and thrilling day I have experienced. Our microchemists isolated pure element 94 (plutonium) for the first time. It is the first time that element 94 has been beheld by the eye of man," said Glenn Seaborg (Metallurgical Laboratory, University of Chicago, August 20, 1942).

Another zealot pointed out the early second period 6–0 shots on goal disparity and related that statistic to the warped affirmation of a Rangers victory. The Zelig was simply not feeling it and attempted to parry the continued feeling of what Harvard PhD Tal Ben-Shahar had dubbed the "arrival fallacy" in his book *Happier.*

The theory can be supported by science wherein the brain is known to release a hormone dopamine, which is linked to happiness, "in anticipation of reward." The doctrine further explains that the arrival fallacy is when the brain is fooled into behaving as if the goal had been reached and subsequently released the soothing hormone. Since the accomplishment has apparently already been reached, the dopamine begins to drop off before it otherwise would. So, if, when the goal is accomplished, the feeling is not only not satisfying but could also materialize as apathy, disappointment, or emptiness.

The Zelig continued to engage in the hockey exchange and made a deliberate effort not to play the role of a chief buzz kill. However, as the levels of unbridled enthusiasm persisted, the Zelig could not resist to remind about the perils of *The Milkmaid and Her Pail.*

A milkmaid had been out to milk the cows and was returning from the field with the shining milk pail balanced nicely on her head. As she walked along, her pretty head was busy with plans for the days to come.

"This good, rich milk," she mused, "will give me plenty of cream to churn. The butter I make I will take to market, and with the money I get for it, I will buy a lot of eggs for hatching. How nice it will be when they are all hatched, and the yard is full of fine young chicks. Then when May day comes, I will sell them, and with the money, I'll buy a lovely new dress to wear to the fair. All the young men will look at me. They will come and try to make love to me—but I shall very quickly send them about their business!"

As she thought of how she would settle that matter, she tossed her head scornfully, and down fell the pail of milk to the ground. And all the milk flowed out, and with it, vanished butter and eggs and chicks and new dress and all the milkmaid's pride.

Do not count your chickens before they are hatched.

A boisterous clucking advanced from the ice surface. The defenseman Beukeboom was slow to the bench after a low check appeared to hyperextend his knee. There was no penalty called. As play resumed, the captain Messier was checked as he skated to retrieve a loose puck. The illegal interference act by the Canucks' Brown knocked the stick from the captain and signaled for the referee Gregson to asses a penalty. A make-up call, the Canucks argued. But nevertheless, the Rangers were awarded a power play. With the first period success of the Messier, Graves, Kovalev unit, Kennan went right back to them.

However, the man advantage did not last long as the Rangers were called for a tripping penalty. The Canucks retained puck possession, and so the call was delayed until the point where the Rangers would regain possession. The Vancouver team was shrewd, and the goalie McClean raced from his position so that the Canucks could add an additional skater. It was hockey's version of all reward and no risk in that as soon as a Ranger touched the puck, the play would be called dead, and the penalty assessed.

The Rangers appeared to be caught off guard by the maneuver, and by the time their captain Linden was closing in on Richter—with Leetch tailing—the outcome was unmistakable.

Canucks score and the two-goal lead was halved—2–1, Rangers.

Most of the suite attendees had not even observed the tally. The party trumped the play. The Zelig thanked the hosts and informed them that he was heading back out to mingle with the gpop. Mark, the intern, clutched the Zelig before his departure and returned the press pass. He thanked him heartily for the opportunity, and the Zelig knew he was referring to the intriguing hookup connection more so than the game.

"Glad you could come with," the Zelig recalled responding. "Just make sure you answer the bell for work tomorrow!"

With over twelve minutes having elapsed in the second period, the Zelig located a neat vantage point to take in action. A section designated for the print media was insulated from the fans and a where security guard held post to the entrance. The Zelig walked past the guard briskly and stood just next to the last occupied seat. A brief glance from someone seated in the section was matched with a slight affirmative yet completely groundless head nod by the Zelig.

Time for hockey.

> A leader is like a shepherd. He stays behind the flock, letting the most nimble go out ahead, whereupon the others follow, not realizing that all along they are being directed from behind. (Nelson Mandela)

The captain Messier and the coach Keenan huddled on the bench following the Canucks' goal. Their alternating nods appeared to signify both were on the same wavelength.

The Rangers had clearly been pressing the action throughout the game, obviously attempting to obtain the early lead and keep the pressure on their opponent to play catch-up. The strategy was successful, but nonetheless, the club found themselves in a familiar position of holding on to the lead.

In the successive moments after Linden's score, the Rangers top line—including Messier—received limited ice time. Instead, it was the checking line of MacTavish, Noonan, and Tikkanen that drew the assignments. Those players effectively slowed the pace and the Canucks momentum. An intermittent Canucks flurry and shot attempt were turned aside by Richter.

The strategy was practical as the Canucks' play appeared to become careless as they pursued both the opposing team and the crusade to regain the energy they held just a few moments earlier. Messier and his line entered for a quick shift and exited quickly after the captain won a face-off in the Rangers' zone. Coach Kennan used the opportunity to change the pace and tapped the line of Kovalev, Matteau, and Larmer. That unit applied prompt and sustained pressure. They swarmed McClean and fired rubber in his direction from all angles. And while none of the bids were actually "on-goal," the game plan had its rewards.

Both Rangers' forwards Kovalev and Larmer were yanked to the ice by Vancouver players Babych and Courtnall respectively. The referee Gregson chose Babych to serve the time for the crime.

Rangers power play. Enter Messier.

> A good leader motivates, doesn't mislead, doesn't exploit (Proverbs 16:10).

The captain won the face-off to begin the two-minute man advantage. And while the Canucks initially cleared the puck, the resultant rush was quick and tight. The defenseman Zubov gained control of the enemy zone. He faked a shot and passed to his right for his forward Noonan. Noonan found a slashing Graves with a pass in front of McClean, and Graves took a swipe at it. While his teammates were performing so productively, Messier found his quiet place directly to McClean's stick side.

> Suddenly I turned around and she was standin' there / With silver bracelets on her wrists and flowers in her hair / She walked up to me so gracefully and took my crown of thorns
>
> Come in, she said / I'll give ya shelter from the storm. (Bob Dylan, "Shelter from the Storm")

Messier's delicate little push directed the puck through McClean and provoked a garden party. The fans were on board. Not only had they regained the two-goal lead, but it was Messier, who provided for them, and it was the comfort that the coach and the captain's leadership and strategy had worked. The Zelig left the perch with his fellow press colleagues and headed toward the green seats for period three.

The Final Twenty
The Summit

> It is not the mountain we conquer but ourselves.
> (Edmund Hillary)

Coupling with TD to start the third period at the green seats was like easing into a warm swimming pool. The muscles relaxed and the mind cleared.

The Zelig filled in the fans, seated in the section, with his travelogue and described the Steven McDonald moment. Unfortunately, but not surprisingly, there were no vacant seats in the section. The Zelig asked those around him if they would mind if he would remain in the aisle crouched adjacent to TD's end seat. There were no protests, and so the Zelig squatted low as the skaters prepared for the start of the period.

The usher's motioning initially eluded the Zelig and TD. It was not until someone gained the Zelig's attention before he noticed the beckoning finger.

"Tell him to fuck off," said TD.

The Zelig casually approached the usher. There was no banter.

"You know you can't block the aisle like that?"

The Zelig replied definitively to the rhetorical question, "I was just catching up with a friend before I have to go back to work."

The usher glanced quickly at the press pass as if glimpsing a solar eclipse.

"Because we hear about it if the aisles are blocked."

"Of course," the Zelig agreed. He turned and waved at TD.

"What the fuck?" TD motioned to the usher. "C'mon!"

The Zelig smiled at the usher before heading down the ramp and back into oblivion.

According to excerpts from the *Glastenbury Wilderness*, there are suspected locales where people have reportedly vanished.

Bennington Triangle is a nickname given by paranormal author Joseph A. Citro to denote an area of southwestern Vermont within which many people have disappeared.

A few of the more notable disappearances include the following:

Middie Rivers was serving as a mountain guide in the area. He was guiding his group back to their camp. He got ahead of the bunch and was never seen again. Police and volunteers searched for the man, but no clue to his fate was ever found.

Paula Welden, a college student, went hiking on the Long Trail one day. She was never seen again, and no trace of her has ever been found.

Paul Jepson an eight-year-old went missing. His scent was followed by dogs, but it was lost on a highway. Frieda Lander disappeared when she was hiking with her cousin. Frieda had separated with her cousin to head back to camp to change after getting her clothes wet, but she never returned to the camp. A massive search was mounted by police, volunteers, firemen, and military sought the woman, but nothing turned up until the following May. Her body was found in a field that had been searched extensively in the previous months.

The Zelig debated whether to return to the print media section but was motivated to remain closer to the greens. He decided, instead, to revert to traversing the exterior concourse which circled the Garden. No triangles, please!

> I went to a garden party / To reminisce with my old friends
> A chance to share old memories / And play our songs again. (Ricky Nelson, "Garden Party")

The Garden soiree was raging as the period began.

"Let's go, Rangers!" The refrain echoed repeatedly like Muzak in a retail store.

The only interruption was the blare of the bugle call. "Charge!"

The Zelig walked briskly as the venue's heart beat matched his own. He observed the action as would a film director attempting to record a difficult to accomplish tracking shot.

The stalwart defenseman Beukeboom had not returned to action. The Rangers opened with a pairing of Lowe and Zubov. The Canucks tried to take advantage of the wounded. They bolted out of the gate like an anxious thoroughbred. "And they're off!"

The Rangers remained fortified in the resistance. After two minutes of frenetic activity, a welcomed whistle put a halt to the contest. It was evident, however, that the Rangers were not going to survive by narrowing their strategy to exclusively playing defense.

> Standing on the defensive indicates insufficient strength; attacking, a superabundance of strength. (Sun Tzu, *The Art of War*)

The Zelig detected a commotion in the lower bowl. The New York Knicks' defensive stalwart Mason was fraternizing with the fanatics. His image was displayed on the scoreboard.

"Dee-fence! Dee-fence!"

"Meiyou." No, the Chinese military strategist would not approve.

The buzzing assault from the Canadian club was plastering the Rangers. And approximately five minutes into the session, the Rocket, Bure, was grounded by Tikkanen, who had no other choice but to diffuse the Russian as he zoomed cleanly toward Richter. The leader Messier won the draw to start the shorthanded Rangers' stint. Following the Rangers' clearing, the Canucks decisively broke out of their zone in an invasion formation. They easily entered the Rangers' sector and positioned for the incursion.

As the Blueshirts' penalty kill squad scrambled to defend, the Canucks exhibited a dizzyingly display of unity. Three sharp accurate passes between Ronning and Courtnall eventually lead to the clincher. Captain Lindedn had secured his second goal of the game, and the Canucks had—once again—battled to within one lucky bounce of the puck margin.

> The opportunity of defeating the enemy is provided by the enemy himself. (Sun Tzu)

The Zelig had abandoned caution and understood that he had to rejoin TD and the green beret for the conclusion of the conflict.

There were no pleasantries when the Zelig returned to the greens. The usher was not stationed at the ramp opening, and all the fans were standing. The Zelig walked to the seats where TD growled about how the best thing that could have happened to the Rangers was giving up the second goal to affirm the sentiment that they would not have been capable of nursing the lead and playing carefully for fifteen minutes.

However, it was followed by a sudden attack by the Canucks' LaFayette and the resulting stupendous save by the keeper Richter. French Army officer Charles de Gaulle had it right when he said, "You have to be fast on your feet and adaptive, or else strategy is useless."

The Canucks were applying constant pressure to the Rangers' depleted defense corps. The banger Beukeboom had returned to the bench following his injury—but not to the ice. The remaining unit, therefore, was skating extra shifts, and the fatigue was showing.

The Vancouver coach Quinn was outmaneuvering his counterpart Keenan as the Canucks were tapping the puck into the Rangers' zone for the sole purpose of punishing the defenseman with body checks. The blueprint was like a boxer concentrating on their opponent's midsection to soften before striking.

However, Keenan would discover a countermove. It appeared to the Zelig and the fans that the Rangers' veteran MacTavish was intentionally baiting the Canucks' captain (and two-goal scorer) Linden. The two players engaged in a cultured shoving encounter with the intensity of a pair of bargain hunters trying to secure the last discounted merchandise. The referee Gregson, however, saw it differently and penalized both players for roughing. Coach Quinn was understandably outraged as the Rangers, in effect, neutralized a captain with an infantryman.

The tactic was efficient as with four skaters aside, the ice opened, and the Rangers' defensemen would have a two-minute respite from the barrage.

Indeed, a few seconds into the four on four play, the veteran defenseman Lowe unleashed a blister from the blue line that eluded the minder McClean but collided with the post. The clang of the puck kissing the goal pillar ignited the crowd. The close encounter, notwithstanding, the subsequent play produced no threats from either team. And there was more than ten minutes to play.

> Your skin like dawn, Mine like musk
> One paints the beginning of a certain end
> The other, the end of a sure beginning.
> (Maya Angelou, "Passing Time")

Would the Rangers and their ravenous, excitable fan base prefer the remaining clock ticks magically disappear and vault them to their future as Stanley Cup champions? Or would they rather enjoy the ride?

"Let's go, Rangers!"

"We want the Cup!"

The fans, at least, had spoken. Buckle up.

The Rangers, too, had seemingly adopted the philosophy that time was not the enemy but an ally. Their play was indicative of the understanding that, at that point in the game and series, the referees were going to be lenient. Thus, the following few moments of play mirrored a Greco-Roman wrestling clinic. But the indisputable fact remained glaring on the scoreboard clock. The amount of time to endure before the zeros would be illuminated could not elapse without torment.

> You take it on faith, you take it to the heart
> The waiting is the hardest part. (Tom Petty,
> "The Waiting")

Newton's first law in hockey considers, "Friction is very low because ice is slippery and very little blade is in contact with the ice." The second law assigns applied force, "The puck accelerates when a stick makes contact with it." And the third law details, "The puck remains at rest or with constant speed until a player's stick makes contact with the puck to change direction and speed of the puck."

However, none of these irrefutable measures contemplates the impact of the goal posts.

The goal posts shall be kept in position by means of flexible pegs affixed in the ice or floor. The flexible pegs shall be ten inches in length and yellow in color.

The goal posts shall be of approved design and material, extending vertically four feet above the surface of the ice and set six feet apart measured from the inside of the posts. A crossbar of the same material as the goal posts shall extend from the top of one post to the top of the other. The goal posts and crossbar shall be painted in red, and all other exterior surfaces shall be painted in white.

While the post had deprived the Rangers of reestablishing a two-goal cushion on the Lowe shot, Richter's goal pole rescued the Rangers from certain jeopardy.

The Canucks' Gelinas cropped upon the unsuspecting Rangers' goalie as a planted boogeyman in a carnival's "House of Horrors." A beaten Richter desperately resorted to flopping and extending any available limb to obstruct what was sure to be the game-tying goal. The keeper's catching glove flew from his hand unintentionally as Gelinas fired. The puck hit the post. The referee did not call a penalty on Richter's illegal action.

Moments later, disaster nearly struck again. The Vancouver's forward Lafayette charged in on Richter unannounced and unwelcomed.

His well-placed and hotly paced foray seemed ticketed for the back of the net. However, the heavenly clangor of the puck striking the bar was as gratifying a sound as if emanating from the Liberty Bell itself.

Regardless of the Canucks' misfortune, they were the buoyed team. Each player on each shift posed a threat that only the Rangers continued groping, and good luck could thwart. Yet despite the advantage in play, the Canucks' squandered opportunities had, correspondingly, whittled the time to a point where it had converted to a Rangers' edge.

> Time is on my side, yes, it is / Now you all were saying that you want to be free
> But you'll come runnin' back / You'll come runnin' back
> You'll come runnin' back to me. (The Rolling Stones, "Time Is on My Side")

The Rangers had maintained their face-off advantage throughout the game and especially in the third period. The team extracted the optimum benefit from their dominance by milking the clock to give their overworked players enough recovery time. The coach Keenan was deliberate with his home ice advantaged "last line change" and the captain Messier was especially calculated in his preparation time.

The Canucks, in contrast, were rushing and careless with their line changes. The officials had set the tone that those infractions would not be cited unless directly involved in the flow of the game. But Vancouver suffered from the sloppiness and caused the defenseman Brown to send a puck from the ice directly into the crowd.

The Rangers were soliciting a penalty call while the Canucks were pointing to the clock, arguing that time had continued to elapse following the whistle.

The officials huddled outside the game attendant's box to discuss both matters. The Rangers rested and composed themselves while the Canucks skated nervously, expending valuable energy. The rulings favored the team from British Columbia as they deemed, the puck did not leave the ice surface directly, and that the clock did erroneously lose 1.6 seconds.

With less than two minutes remaining, play resumed. All eyes were on the goalie McClean to gauge at what point he would sacrifice his net to allow for an additional Canuck skater. Vancouver had maintained its method of attempting to expose the fatigued Rangers' defensemen by sending the puck into the zone and attacking the retriever. The Rangers were happy to participate and responded by icing the puck. They owned the face-off battle, after all, and clearly did not fear the consequences.

With the recurrent cryptic 1:00 flickering from the clock like a manipulative demonic light, McClean abdicated his throne. The Canucks rushed each of their six skaters into the Rangers' zone. A flurry of activity provoked a fluky yet fleeting crowd reaction. Hushed silence. The sleek defenseman Leetch had displayed his grit by selling out and diving in front of Richter to block a shot. The puck caromed to the rear boards where Zubov cleared. The fans, having rediscovered their lost breath, roared, and the Canucks chased slowly. The whistle and linesman's raised arm signifying a questionable icing call could not diffuse the elation.

"We Will Rock You" was piped through the Garden's sound system but overpowered by the organic and omnipresent "Let's go, Rangers!" and "We want the Cup!" The scoreboard flashed images of the general manager Smith who had made his way behind the Rangers' bench from his eye in the sky perch. The mayor Giuliani was seated nearby with his wife and son. The crowd crowed at his appearance. "Rudy. Rudy."

The Zelig and TD had joined the entire visible crowd by interlocking one type of body part or another as if tandem skydivers. TD bellowed something along the lines of how ignorant the Canucks were playing into the Rangers' dependable draw-winning hands.

The captain Messier, on cue, won another face-off and drew the puck back to Larmer who guided the puck out of the zone and apparently toward the boundary and prospect of a Rangers' cup! But despite a Golden Raspberry award-winning performance by the Canucks' pursuit of the puck, another icing was called. One. Point. Six. Seconds. To. Glorious. Victory.

The players positioned for the final face-off. The Rangers built a human border wall in front of their keeper Richter. The Canucks maintained the extra skater and formed a conga line facing the goal. Only divine intervention could save the Vancouver squad who had demonstrated amazing grace throughout the series.

The Zeilg and TD joined the surrounding fans in jubilant anticipation. The familiar chants had deviated creatively. "We want the Cup!" "Red seats suck!" A throwback that incited the "reds" to turn, bow, and wave sardonically.

"Nineteen forty!" Then, "Nineteen ninety-four!" It was the proper way to end the Rangers arduous passage. The Zelig recalled, pondering. Securing the puck in your own zone in front of your keeper before your fans and for your city—and not watching as the passionately contested yet inanimate object slithered gently away from all the combatants before settling to a resting place in a deserted area of the ice. Yes, the icing call was icing on the cake.

The puck was dropped, and the Garden was lifted. Instantaneously. Fireworks exploded from the iconic ceiling. The players gathered in a circle and jumped onto the very same backs and shoulders they had relied upon to reach the milestone. The fans were feasting on the solidarity of experiencing the unifying achievement. The emotions were induced, not by what could be observed, but rather by what was being absorbed.

The Zelig understood how each fan, whether witnessing or watching, brought their own individual realities to the reality of the moment. It was a compelling dichotomy between sharing publicly what was felt so personally.

TD had continuously pumped high-five palm slaps into the air without regard to connecting. The Zelig recalls the misty eyes of those around him before he could even detect the swell building inside himself. It had been accessible to play the role of the fan and even the friend. But as the Zelig thought of his family and wondered if the wonderful wife had managed to keep the two sons awake to sense the stage as much as any four- and two-year-old could practically understand, the Zelig, the father himself, could feel the sentiment tsunami wash over him.

"Fucking ay," TD shouted. "For you, Fisch!"

"And for you, Alan." The Zelig recollected. The welled tears had lanced the levee protecting those worried about preserving masculinity. So it would be no exaggeration to account for the description of the fan's crying—"Nineteen forty! Nineteen ninety-four!"

A fan in an adjacent section displayed a sign—"Now I Can Die in Peace." TD stood on his green seat and bellowed, "There is a God!" The Zelig asked if TD had seen that sign displayed in the crowd earlier. Following the "What sign?" response, the Zelig searched the lower bowl area for confirmation of something he thought he saw but may have conceived.

The rink was engulfed in a smoky haze from the pyrotechnics. The fog, although, had illuminated the on-ice celebration and not shrouded it as if to belie the beholding eye. The NHL commissioner presented the most valuable playoff player—Leetch—with the Conn Smythe trophy as the unceasing bedlam briefly cooled.

> The cup, the cup itself, from which our Lord Drank at the last sad supper with his own. (Alfred Lord Tennison's *Holy Grail*)

The image of two white-gloved attendants bearing the Stanley Cup and toting the trophy to a platform near center ice invoked the comparisons to the Christian relic.

Blasphemous, maybe, but any such sin must have been forgiven on that night where so many were treating the culmination of the hockey season (of literally fifty-four of them) as a religious experience. The public address announcer introduced the symbol as if its existence was an article of being.

"Ladies and gentlemen, the Stanley Cup!" The commissioner approached the table and paid a brief tribute to the Rangers' organization before announcing the captain Messier and directing him to come get the Stanley Cup.

While the crowd continued its vociferous adulation, the successive passing of the chalice to each deserving member of the 1993–94 New York Rangers was beginning to feel slightly intrusive. While the fans naturally felt as worthy of the reward as the players, the reaction those players exhibited while thrusting the Cup overhead and kissing and skating in circles while cradling the trophy had become evident of the devotion and commitment necessary to reach the summit. An achievement, that while any fan would like to emulate, should properly be reserved for those who earned it on the ice.

The championship team assembled for a series of photos, and some in the crowd had begun to leave their sections. Kevin O. appeared, somehow, from behind TD and the Zelig.

"Amazing, boys," as the Zelig could best summon the spirit of the comment.

The Zelig did recall precisely, however, providing Mark, the intern's press pass and informing Kevin O. that he had hooked up and would not be leaving with us.

"Leaving?" The Zelig recalled Kevin O.'s rhetorical question. "We're just getting started!"

OVERTIME

SALMON, PBRs, AND THE BULLET

The Club

"It just looked like there were way too many people downtown, and it's been out of control."

"What people did to this city and why people act like this, I have no idea."

"A bunch of guys started rocking a car, then they flipped it over, and five minutes later, it was on fire. It was just out of control."

"Police in riot gear and ambulances appeared to be having trouble getting into the trouble zones. The combination of tear gas, pepper spray, and smoke from the fires was choking."

Kevin O. pulled small black decals from his pocket and instructed TD and the Zelig to place them anywhere around the hand and wrist area. The Zelig recalled believing the decals were shaped as aces. He placed his on the wristwatch. The Garden club was going to be the place where Rangers' executives and media members would celebrate the championship with an open bar and free buffet. The black ace decal was the admission secret. The Zelig was following TD's lead on the level of questioning regarding the origins and knowledge of these covert actions since he had been closet to the O family. But TD was more interested in what was happening outside the Garden. The Zelig could understand.

> I guess the thing is that it's not so much that you are confined but just knowing that you can't leave is more aggravating than anything else. (A Minnesota farmer on *Cabin Fever*)

The threesome approached the club and indirectly presented the decals to the gentlemen supervising the clientele flow. Immediately upon entering, TD was questioning anyone who would hear on how the Rangers' fans outside—on the city streets—were reacting to the win. Kevin O. posed the inquiry to whom had to be one of New York's finest enjoying a favorable, plainclothes detail that evening. The response was that the New Yorkers were reportedly reveling heartily but peacefully. However, Vancouver was the different story summarized by the preceding characterizations in this chronicle.

With the curiosity itch sufficiently scratched, it was time to hobknob with the exclusive guests. Unlike the game 7 "must separate" rules of engagement, the trio stuck together and helped themselves to a cocktail and a bite to eat. Standing at a high-top table near the bar, the boys began the bit of casually identifying those in the congregation.

Garden president, Gutkowski, was easy to mark given his silver mane. Was that General Manager Smith perhaps? Are those dudes in the white shirts and baseball caps some of the real Black Aces? Eddie O.? Karpovtsev? Is that the Brawler, Kocur? The mood in the club was convivial but contained and not comparable to the boy's need to spree which burned as belly fire. They decided to forsake caution, the risk of exposure, and ventured from the table to rub elbows.

> Magic's an art where you use sleight of hand or illusion to create wonder. And I was just intrigued with that idea. (David Blaine)

The young boy who approached the trine was exuberant and not the least bit anxious as he immediately dived into a magic routine. Kevin O. smiled weakly and slinked to the bar. The Zelig and TD indulged the fledgling magician as he performed.

After a few courteous remarks of fascination and light applause, the father approached and initially apologized to TD and the Zelig about his son Matthew's intrusion.

"No problem. The kid has a future." The Zelig assumed the approximate response to the father, play-by-play man, Sam Rosen, who departed proudly after the boy had received a few bucks from either (or both) TD and the Zelig.

"Let's hit the bar."

> Why alcohol tolerance is dangerous? Ethanol abuse doesn't result in anything positive, especially when it's combined with ethanol resistance. People who have a tolerance to alcohol drink more of it, and sometimes the amounts they consume can reach a deadly level. (AlcoRehab.org)

The alcohol consumption was having no effect on the Zelig. His pace had been brisk in the brief time at the club since he had zero supply during the game. While TD and Kevin O. discovered the inhibition to circulate, the Zelig remained anchored to the bar. Until nature called.

> Illusion reveals that the brain fills in peripheral vision. What we see in the periphery, just, may sometimes be a visual illusion. (Association for the Psychological Science)

The Zelig's peripheral vision had not created an allusion. He was urinating next to Marv Albert.

The internal debate raged as to whether he should speak. A question? A general remark about the game? A simple, "Hey?" The

Zelig had to say something. How could he live with himself and the memory of the missed opportunity?

> For all sad words of tongue and pen, the saddest
> are these, "It might have been."
> (John Greenleaf Whittier)

"These fans and this organization really do deserve this." The Zelig remembered his baiting proclamation.

"Yes," Marv Albert replied.

The Zelig had accomplished the goal—a "Yes" from Marv Albert. He would have been thrilled had the exchange ended where, this, his anticipated future lifelong story had begun. But Marv was not finished.

"What publication?" he posed, motioning to the NHL press pass.

What publication, indeed? The question might as well have been about the topical Civil War in Rwanda or the Serbian attacks on Bosnia for any possible intelligent or truthful reply.

The Zelig and the college roommate, TD, were asked by the proprietor of the establishment hosting Spring Fest 1981 if they knew of the exhibitionist standing nude atop a barnlike structure and prattling at the students below.

Lumbo had mysteriously appeared at the State University of New York school situated off the shores of Lake Ontario for the spring semester. He hailed from EI, and while having earned a reputation for creative partying, he had apparently added the self-display to his routine for the new Central New York audience. Lumbo's naked merriment had reached such levels that the dormitory, which he resided and where TD had also been recently elected as president, had circulated a petition for those who would confirm having seen the private parts firsthand. The petition would be used as grounds for Lumbo's expulsion.

The day arrived where college representatives, including the dorm director, Marge, would meet to discuss the Lumbo situation.

TD would be present as a representative, and the Zelig was asked to make sure the accused would attend. Moments before the scheduled hearing, the Zelig was frantically searching the dorm rooms, including those of his future wonderful wife, in the hunt for the great white whale.

Having failed to locate Lumbo, the Zelig ran down to the conference room area in the basement of the dorm where the inquisition would take place. Upon arrival, Lumbo's appearance was so staggering. The Zelig looked away as if fearing an identical result of having gazed directly into the eyes of Medusa.

Snorkel goggles.

A flotation belt.

A prop rubber knife.

Swim fins.

And nothing else.

Recovering from the shock, the Zelig raced toward the entrance. Lumbo kicked the door open and entered. The gathering nervously gasped and shrieked at the form before them.

"Hey, who moved the pool?"

The Zelig heard Lumbo's psychotic witticism as he darted into the room and reached for a stack of paper placed on a nearby table. He scanned the pages of the paper he had used to cloak the madman's manhood. Looking down to admire his emergency cover-up, the Zelig's peripheral vision could clearly capture the newspaper's banner.

"The *Oswegonian*," the Zelig eventually responded to Marv Albert's inquiry somehow retrieving the Lumbo memory to cite the independent student newspaper of Oswego State.

The Locker Room

The Zelig was overcome with nerves. The time spent in the Garden club was short. The guests were rustling, and a few had exited the room. Kevin O.'s command for TD and the Zelig to assemble was abrupt. The thirty-minute party was unique and provided the

Zelig with stories to tell. But even with the end in sight, the Zelig knew he had experienced a slice of history and was thrilled until Kevin O. whispered.

"We're going down to the locker room."

While a list of questions entered the Zelig's mind, TD was as excited as a prospective contestant on the old *Let's Make a Deal* game show. "Pick me, Monty! Pick me!"

Kevin O.'s instructions were concise. They would follow a few of the departing Garden club guests to the elevators and tail them to the destination. The Zelig swallowed his questions before they could leave his throat.

"How do we know they're going to the locker room?"

"How are we going to get in?"

"What do we do when we're in? Am I going to have to fake an interview?"

The small group huddled outside a remote elevator bank. The Zelig stared down at his shoes to avoid eye contact. TD, in contrast, was fidgety and loud.

The awareness of drawing attention was nonexistent. He chatted with others and shared his excitement about the unbelievable opportunity. Kevin O. lurked silently and smiled at the exchange.

One of the two elevator doors opened, and an attendant stepped out. The group hustled in. The Zelig walked behind Kevin O. and occupied a corner spot. He touched the lanyard discretely as if to ask whether the press pass was the ticket in. Kevin O. acknowledged.

The Zelig turned his attention to TD. He was beaming and clapping and hooting with enthusiasm. There was no NHL press pass around his neck.

The elevator attendant explained to a club party guest how the players were completing the on-ice ceremonies and press conferences and would be entering the locker room shortly. The doors opened, and the rank filed out. TD pushed his way toward the front, but Kevin O. lagged. The Zelig remained behind, and TD backtracked.

Kevin O. explained that while the press pass and the black decals would get them in, there was a possibility that they would be checked against a list. If that were to happen, he reassured, follow his lead.

The corridor leading to the locker room was narrow. The Zelig was surprised at the outdated decorum. It was obvious the millions spent on the Garden renovation was not targeted for the bowels or to enhance the comfort of the Ringling Brother's circus who had, for dozens of years, called the Garden, "home." The Zelig made the effort to avoid overtly surveying the surroundings. He attempted to act "put out" and distracted even while his palms leaked with sweat and heart fluttered.

Two security guards were stationed outside the locker room doors. They were the outsized gentleman, bodyguards, or bouncers. The Zelig watch closely as those in front of the line entered. He didn't observe a list or even a hint of what credentials were inspected. Certainly, the NHL press pass dangling from his neck would suffice.

They inched toward the door. TD was craning his neck for a peek inside and looked back to the Zelig with a broad knowing grin. One of the guards stepped inside. His partner moved in front of the doorway and held his hand out. Stop.

A voice from the back of the line stated that the team was approaching. The Zelig assumed that the window was closed and that they had missed the opportunity. But the guards assumed their post, and the line moved.

Kevin O. casually tapped one of the guards on the arm as he passed. Slick move. TD followed and provided a verbal greeting while displaying his black ace decal. The guards didn't acknowledge nor detain, and TD was in. The Zelig felt the urge to lift the pass from his sternum as he walked between the guards, but he settled for a clumsy, above the waist body pivot. The security professional continued to stare straight away while indiscreetly motioning with his left hand to keep the line moving.

The Zelig was in the New York Rangers' locker room. The area was cramped and outmoded. A stained, drop-ceiling created the mood of a basement high school drinking party. Those in the room appeared busy. A few clubhouse attendants were dumping gear into large canvass bins as media representatives were prepping. TD ran to the Zelig. He was exuberant and ticking off the players he was most interested in seeing. Kevin O., the Zelig had noticed, had either perfectly camouflaged himself or found the perfect secure vantage point.

TD informed the Zelig that he was going back toward the main entrance to gain a clearer perspective for when the players arrived. The Zelig opted to move toward a corner near a bank of cubicle-sized lockers.

A bright light bank caught the Zelig's eyes in the area he had targeted. The Zelig walked behind a gentleman positioning the lights and placed his back against a white brick wall with red- and blue-painted stripes. He looked up and saw the label adhesive "Leetch." It was the Conn Smythe winner's locker.

Clothing and gear either hung from small hooks or were strewn on the floor. The Zelig momentarily contemplated helping himself to a keepsake. *Something small*, he thought—even a roll of athletic tape. Larceny was not the motivation. He wanted validation. What would be the point of these unbelievable circumstances if no one would believe him? The Zelig reached for the top shelf with his eye on a puck situated next to the tape and near a line of elbow pads.

The voice was startling. The Zelig froze. He turned and gazed at the lights. A few seats had been set up to presumably facilitate an interview. Two men were motioning and speaking loudly. The Zelig recognized a voice and the face. The thoughts of pinching were gone. An act of intervention, the Zelig had later come to believe. He moved toward ESPN's Steve Levy as if he was a dear friend.

"Class of '83," the Zelig stated.

Levy glanced but did not respond. He continued his preparation.

The Zelig pressed, "Laker hockey. Romney Field House."

The Oswego college references caught Levy's ears, and he smiled.

The Zelig lifted the press pass and joked, "The *Oswegonian*."

Levy chuckled, but his body language sent a clear signal that he was a man on a job. For the Zelig, however, the exchange was an epiphany. He had been trying to adopt a concealed "fly on the wall" approach when the entire time he felt as conspicuous as a wasp in an empty can.

But the ironic inspiration of using an *Oswegonian* reference to both Marv Albert and Steve Levy in the locations and circumstances of the adventure was liberating.

The Ranger players rushed into the locker room as if labored swimmers finally reaching their shoreline destination. The Zelig could recall how quickly the place heated up. He moved away from the Leetch/Levy corner as the players converged onto their lockers. Legitimate media members congregated around Graves and Richter to record their thoughts and comments. The Zelig spotted TD in the opposite corner, adjacent to the training room.

"It's Mess." TD pointed.

Messier was getting treatment on his legs. The Zelig recalled detecting how exhausted the captain appeared. He seemed hollow and drained. Those surrounding the leader were careful to obstruct a clear view into the area. But TD wanted his man and yelled a few "You're the man, Mess!" sentiments.

The room continued to fill as the professionals from the Garden club entered with the players. Rosen and Trautwig were interviewing. Levy was commenting. The Zelig wondered if he saw Sal "Red Light" Messina or maybe Howie Rose in one corner? The open space was shrinking rapidly as would the impact of flood waters in a low-lying area. But there was nothing else flowing. No champagne. And no sign of the Cup.

The Zelig also sensed the strange phenomenon of how the volume in the room would increase before the subsequent wave of people entered. He surmised it could have been an echo from the corridor. But within minutes of the player barrage, the locker room was a babel of pandemonium.

The Zelig's memory of whether he first saw Graves or detected TD's familiar bellow "Adam Bomb!" was uncertain. But the reflection of setting eyes upon the Cup for the first time was vivid. Graves was holding the chalice close to his body and kissing the rim.

The sweat pouring from under his Stanley Cup Champions cap glistened against the silver. Photographers swooped in to capture the image, and the Zelig could clearly see TD standing directly behind Graves, smiling as if flirting with a girl at a junior high school social.

The Cup's debut garnered the frenetic attention of a beaming debutante's entrance. The shoulder-to-shoulder locker room crowd whirled behind the trophy's path as if leaves blew forcefully by sporadic wind gusts. It was at that point when the booze arrived. Spritzes of champagne and beer sprayed the room as if from the trail of a fireworks display. And any remnants of the Zelig's prior paranoiac trepidation had vanished in a puff of smoke.

The jubilee had appeared to transform, in the Zelig's perspective, into a family party. The players were calling names from across the room and instructing groups of cohorts to assemble. The Zelig was caught in the undertow of one of these groups. He didn't fight the current and moved briskly with the others.

The identification of Rangers' Glenn Anderson and Jay Wells was certain. The Zelig's, honest recall, however, was not total. Wells was handling the Cup as if it were weightless. He lowered it and began pouring canned beer into the spout.

As the discarded cans clanked onto the floor, the Zelig spotted a familiar red, white, and blue design. Either the Rangers had brewed and bottled their own ale for the occasion, or Jay Wells was filling the Stanley Cup with the foamy suds of Pabst Blue Ribbon. Wells lifted and tilted.

The 1982 Edmonton Oilers' roster was "dripping" with future hall of fame players, including Wayne Gretzky. The team would eventually achieve dynasty status by ending the dynasty of the New York Islanders, who had won four consecutive Stanley Cups between 1980 and 1983.

However, the '82 Oilers were not there yet. The team supported the great one Greztky with a cast familiar to Rangers' fans—Messier, Glen Anderson, and Kevin Lowe. The hockey club had advanced to the Smythe Division semifinals where they faced the Los Angeles Kings. The best-of-five series was tied at one game apiece when the teams met for game 3 on April 10 in Los Angeles at The Forum—the Kings' home on Manchester Boulevard.

The Kings were a confident team, having bested the Oilers in a wild 10–8 series-opening victory in Edmonton before suffering a 3–2 overtime loss in game 2. The Oilers were dominant, however, in the third game and led 5–0 entering the third period.

Jay Wells, the Kings' twenty-two-year-old defenseman who had scored one goal on the season, managed to put a puck past the Oilers' Grant Fuhr with just over two minutes into the final frame. The innocuous goal appeared to only annoy the Oilers as it ended the shutout bid. As history would write, however, the Wells goal triggered the Kings' coup as they scored five times to tie the game before winning 6–5 in overtime. It was the greatest comeback in the history of the Stanley Cup playoffs.

The Zelig believed he heard Wells blurt, "Miracle on Manchester!" and motioning to his current teammate but former opponent Anderson before the quaff. The beer trickled from the corners of his mouth as he gulped. He lowered the sacred symbol of excellence and filled 'er up again! The Zelig saw Glenn Anderson escort someone into the circle and thought he heard garbled shouts about the "salmon sandwiches!"

A rousing cheer proliferated the locker room. The woman was standing next to the Zelig. Jay Wells handed the Cup to Anderson. He sipped from it slowly appearing to avoid striking its rim against the gouge on his nose. Wells stepped in for another wave of the PBR's. Anderson lifted the Cup and allowed the woman to sample its spoils.

She placed both hands firmly around the spout as Anderson secured the base. She took a quick swig and raised her arm triumphantly. The Zelig was next. He clutched Lord's Stanley Cup from whom he had every reason to believe was the salmon sandwich maker herself, Ann Anderson, and widened his mouth to allow the beer that made Milwaukee famous to cross his lips.

The Zelig could understand how Jay Wells was handling the Cup as if weightless for he too had no perception of its heft. While conscious of having the prized possession in his hands, there was no fear of dropping the trophy, only the joy of participating in one of sports most honored traditions. Lowering the Cup from his mouth, the Zelig passed it to his right. Selfishly, he didn't pay attention to the next gentleman's turn at history. Instead, the Zelig slowly stepped back just outside the human circle.

The deep breaths were helpful in assigning perspective to the experience. The Zelig did not feel privileged or lucky. His minor stabs of guilt had also subsided. He no longer feared being exposed as an imposter nor did he feel any of the sentimentality that overcame him at the game's conclusion. Maybe, the Zelig surmised, his clarity of thought was because—right smack in the heart of chaos—he was experiencing solitude. And the state of isolation could conjure only one prevailing emotion—exhilaration. Feeling the need to share the moment, the Zelig went searching for TD.

> Today I became King of the Court w/out a diamond-encrusted crown thrust upon my sweaty head. Instead my markings of royalty were the t-shirt draping my body like a robe soaked in champagne & the pain in my right knee—a sign of a battle endured, my will tested & bested by none as the ball flew off my hands as swift as an arrow toward the heart of a target—my fingers ringless yet feeling like gold. (Jacob Saenz, "Holding Court")

The captain was holding court near the locker room's training area. TD was listening attentively as one of Messier's loyal zealots. The Zelig approached slowly trying to avoid disruption. He could hear TD in chortling agreement to all the leader's proclamations and recognized his friend's innate ability to harmonize in that setting. Although, upon further reflection, the Zelig wondered if TD's aptitude was more a product of learned behavior through similar experiences.

Baseball fans were debating whether the heavy rains on Sunday, October 26, 1986, that postponed game 7 of the World Series would favor the visiting Red Sox or the home Mets. The Red Sox had snatched defeat from the jaws of victory with the ten-inning loss in game 6 on Saturday night. The series clincher had been scheduled for Sunday, but the inclement weather pushed the finale to Monday night.

TD gladly accepted Mike O.'s invitation to attend the deciding game via the magic bean MLB press passes he obtained through the father's PBA connections.

> The best laid schemes o' mice an' men
> Gang aft a-gley. (Robert Burns, "To a Mouse")

TD was tossed from game 7 before its conclusion through either carelessness or recklessness.

Regardless, having had his credentials revoked by security, he found himself outside Shea Stadium where he came across ticket scalpers. He bought his way back in. Hurrying through the main concourse, TD ran into Met legend Ron Swoboda. TD proceeded to tell his tale to the, most likely disinterested, 1969 World Series hero.

As the story went, Swoboda gave TD his diamond club press pass. TD ultimately parlayed the pass to gain access to the Mets' locker room following their 8–5 World Series-clinching victory over the Red Sox.

So while the marvel of participating in the Rangers' triumph presented the Zelig a multitude of thoughts, feelings, and rationalizations, celebration scamming was old hat for TD.

Kevin O. sidled to the Zelig, and they both monitored TD's interaction with Messier. The Zelig shared his Cup drinking anecdote.

"Classic," Kevin O. responded. "Now let's get him out of here. We've got another stop."

The Auction House

> January 8, 1902, an inbound express train from Connecticut stopped in the tunnel at Fifty-sixth Street, waiting for clearance into Grand Central. It was snowing, and a local from White Plains, despite warning signals as far back as Sixty-third Street, crashed into the express, shredding its two rear passenger cars. Firefighters who climbed down into the tunnel found a panorama of horrors.
>
> Fifteen were killed, thirty-six injured. The engineer of the local, John M. Wisker, thirty-six, said that he had not been able to see the signals. He said that this was a frequent condition and that he always uttered a prayer when he entered the tunnels but was afraid to complain to the railroad.
>
> On January 24, a coroner's jury exonerated Wisker and declared that the railroad was responsible. But Wisker was discharged by the railroad in February and was indicted by the district attorney for manslaughter in March, despite the decision of the coroner's jury.
>
> He was found not guilty in April 1903 after a jury trial.

> No railroad officials were punished, but in the following year, 1903, the state legislature mandated the conversion from steam to electric power. The first electric engine went into service in 1906, and the change was completed in 1907. There was no plaque or memorial at the site of the 1902 disaster, no trace of the event that changed so many lives and so much of New York. (Christopher Gray, *New York Times*)

It was not easy peeling away from the locker room scene. The area outside the Garden continued to throb. The group was joined by Mike O.

"The after party is at the Auction House," he proclaimed. "We're invited."

New York City travel safety had come a long way since the early 1900s. But on that June night in 1994, and the Manhattan streets gridlocked, the Zelig had no idea how they were going to get from Thirty-Third and Eighth to the Auction House on Eighty-Ninth and Second without encountering their own "panorama of horrors."

The Auction House earned its name because most of its furniture and art came from the auction houses that owner and operator, Johnny B. Barounis, frequented throughout the northeast. The bar was considered a "diamond in the rough" with a parlor or lounge persona where people could escape the chaos of the city. The Auction House had a sense of mystery and privacy, suggesting that patrons of the bar "had to know about it" (*Manhattan Sideways*).

An odd location for a New York Rangers Stanley Cup Championship after-party, the Zelig mused. But, hey, if Mike O. claimed we had an invitation, who was he to argue? However, given the congestion, the minor detail of traveling both up and crosstown remained cryptic.

The yellow taxi pulled curbside without having been hailed. Mike O. rushed to the passenger side window and spoke to the driver.

"This is us, boys," he crowed and hopped into the front seat. The boys packed into the back.

On route to the Auction House, Mike O. was demanding details of the evening. In response to the accounts, his naughty smirk had developed into appreciative snickers.

The ride was going unexpectedly smoothly when the police presence was observed near Central Park. The driver inched toward the blockade, and an officer approached, motioning to lower the window.

"Where are you headed?" he asked.

"Auction House. Upper East Side," the driver responded.

"You're going to have to turn around." The officer pointed. "Fifty-Seventh Street."

Mike O. leaped from the passenger seat and walked around the front of the cab. He and the officer moved away from the vehicle as they conversed.

"Probably better off," the Zelig recalled expressing the sentiment.

"Fuck that," TD most likely countered. "We're getting there."

Mike O. returned to the cab. He jumped into the passenger seat. The officer motioned for the driver to continue. He waved as we passed. Mike O. returned the gesture. TD was clapping and hooting. Kevin O. glanced fleetingly at the Zelig. "Don't ask."

Yorkville, the Upper East Side neighborhood known for its amiable residential character and homey attitude, was sleeping. As the cab moved past the flowery Ruppert Park on Ninetieth Street, the recognition that it was well after midnight and on a weeknight was pronounced. Most normal people had been in bed for hours, resting from life's daily routine and not carousing, celebrating a Stanley Cup championship.

And then they came upon Second Avenue.

The driver attempted to make his right hand turn onto the avenue for the remaining one block excursion to the Auction House. A New York City police officer, standing beside a small barricade, had another idea.

"Road's closed. You can take Ninetieth to York," he instructed.

"Okay, boys, we're on foot," Mike O. proclaimed.

The crew exited the cab as Mike O. settled with the driver and walked south on Second Avenue. The placid neighborhood was suddenly wired. A meager barrier closed the corner of Eighty-Ninth Street where another of New York's finest stood guard.

As Mike O. spoke to the officer, TD shuffled forward and pointed to the assemblage. The street was sealed from its surrounding avenues, and people were milling civilly.

"This way." Mike O. was the general.

As his soldiers, the men followed dutifully just as George Washington's 1776 Continental Army had, defeating the British at the Battle of Harlem Heights—a historic area within the Yorkville section.

> Ambition is the path to success. Persistence is the vehicle you arrive in. (Bill Bradley)

A younger Zelig was faced with a career path choice. Link, a college suitemate who had also met his version of the wonderful wife at school, informed the Zelig that his wife could get him overnight shifts at Sports Phone.

976-1313—the number desperate fans could call for information and brief sixty-second scores and updates. Got a dime? Call Sports Phone. Not only had the gambler's dream spawned future media studs, such as "Matteau, Matteau, Matteau" Howie Rose but also forced local cable stations, such as the Madison Square Garden Network, to launch the *Sports Desk*.

The Bullet Bob Page manned the MSG Network's *Sports Desk* during the early-mid-1990s. A Michigan native, his sarcastic and satirical style did not sit well with some New York sports fans.

He once criticized a New York Rangers' player swap with "Talk about trading Tweedle Dee for Tweedle Dumb." Page was on air, behind his sports desk, providing updates for game 7.

The Zelig, ultimately, chose a non-sports-related career path. While he had achieved some level of success in his professional field, he occasionally speculated on how his life would have turned out given the alternate route.

The Auction House was invisible. The crowd had formed outside its clandestine entrance but was segregated by an ad hoc, parallel playpen construction that extended south from the upscale lounge to the brick townhouses across Eighty-Sixth Street.

A line of people amassed inside the playpen facing the Auction House. A security guard was positioned near the Second Avenue coordinate, and another was posted near the doorway. Mike O. spoke to the first security guard.

"There is a guest list."

"We're on it."

"Okay, go ahead, but if you're not on the list, you're gone. You can hang here." He motioned to the street.

"We're on it."

We proceeded to the Auction House. Standing in front of us was the Bullet, himself. A few spectators recognized Bob Page.

"Bullet! Bullet!"

He waved and smiled. He approached security and provided his name. The sentry scanned the clipboard.

"I'm sorry. Name, again, please?"

The "Bullet" shout-outs intensified.

"Bob Page. MSG Network. I work for the team."

"I'm sorry, sir, I don't have you listed."

The Zelig would never embarrass an accomplished professional such as Bob Page. This account is intended to simply relay the most accurate recollection of events. But the Bullet was snubbed. He stormed into the crowd unappreciative of the mocking—"Bullet. Bullet. Bullet."

The men from EI were up. Mike O. whispered the name forcefully. The guard quickly glanced at his list and smiled.

"And they're with me," Mike O. added.

"Enjoy, gentlemen."

The red-carpet ride continued.

Rembrandt and De Goya reproductions hung from exposed brick walls. Velvet curtains, ornate mirrors, and soothing light gave the place a museum vibe. Where's the bar? And where are the Rangers?

> Byrdes of on kynde and color flok and flye always together. (William Turner, 1545, *Rescuing of Romish Fox*)

The Zelig had found a friend at the Auction House. Steve Larmer had set himself furtively at the corner of the lounge. The previously suppressed alcohol reaction the Zelig had experienced had ignited into a flaming flambé. He was the bar bigwig ordering rounds of shots for all his friends, including Larmer.

The veteran Ranger was a mellow cat. He spoke honestly about the thrill of winning for the New York fans and how he rose from humble NHL beginnings being a low-draft pick and working his way through juniors in Niagara Falls. For the first time since the Garden club party, the Zelig did not feel intimidated. The comfort level was so acute that the Zelig would protect Larmer's personal space as the Auction House crowd intensified.

"Hey, relax, give my boy Stevie some space here, man." The Zelig loved to have relived that moment with those words.

He belonged. The night's gravity had finally turned to levity.

"Shots for all my friends!"

Coincidently, on the outskirts of a drape-enclosed room, TD was partying with Tikkanen. The hell-raiser from Helsinki was in possession of the Cup. The "Grate One," as Tikkanen had been dubbed by his Oiler teammates, was commandeering patron's drinks and emptying into the Cup. TD assumed the role has his plus one and scampered through the chic confines of the Auction House swiping and draining drinks.

The bustle caught the attention of not only those lucky insiders but also from the growing group of fans huddled on Eighty-sixth Street.

"We want the Cup! We want the Cup!"

Tik lowered the Cup and sipped the overflowing alcohol from its brim. Ditto, TD from the opposite side creating the facsimile of the *Lady and the Tramp* sharing a spaghetti string. He lifted the trophy and scooted from the bar onto the street. The Cup's appearance with the liquid mix spilling from its lip sent the crowd into a frenzy.

"The Cup. The Cup. We want the Cup!"

Tikkanen hoisted and ran around the periphery of the playpen. The fans rushed to the edge to pat the chalice as it passed. TD joined the pageantry and followed the Ranger champion like a pilot fish. He pumped his fist skyward taking in the adulation as if it were for him. Perhaps it was, the Zelig mused as he and his pal Larmer watched, between shots, from their intimate little bar spot.

Perhaps, in the end, it was all for the fans like the boys from EI.

The Zelig could not be certain if the choice to end the day/night/morning with a meal at Sarge's had any connection to the Mike O. connection. Abe Katz, a former New York City police officer who worked the Murray Hill beat for twenty-five years, opened the establishment in 1964 following his retirement. The history was a mystery. However, as thirty years later, the ravenous boys were destroying the menu and commemorating on their shared adventure.

When with her clouds the early dawn illumes
Our doubtful streets, wistful they grow and mild
As if a sleeping soul grew happy and smiled,
The whole dark city radiantly blooms.
Pale spires lift their hands above the glooms
Like a resurrection, delicately wild,
And flushed with slumber like a little child,
Under a mist, shines forth the innocent Tombs.
Thus have I seen it from a casement high.
As unsubstantial as a dream it grows.
Is this Manhattan, virginal and shy,
That in a cloud so rapturously glows?
Ethereal, frail, and like an opening rose,
I see my city with an enlightened eye. (Anna Hempstead Branch, "New York at Sunrise")

The Zelig parted. TD and the O brothers were heading home. The Zelig had a different destination. He began his walk south on

Broadway. The physical sensations of the escapade remained fresh. He tried to push them away to clear his mind, but they were gummy and vibrant. The one-man Broadway parade—the Zelig continued his solitary course with the rising sun in the forefront.

"Johnny Mazz!"

The voice was distinctly TD's. It was not a calling. It was a cheer.

The Zelig thought about turning to respond. But what words were left? What actions could punctuate the moment?

He concluded with a simple arm raise and extension of the right index finger.

Number one.

"Johnny Mazz!" The encore.

The Zelig reached into his pocket. He clipped his work identification badge to his trousers' belt loop. John Mazzullo, Employee ID 714509.

John Mazzullo was walking to work. Just as the New York Rangers had done—he had to answer the bell.

POSTGAME

CANYON OF HEROES

There are eight million stories in the naked city.
This has been one of them.

—The Naked City

On June 17, 1994, more than one million people attended the New York Rangers' parade.

The Zelig and TD scammed their way to ride on the Mark Messier float as showers of shredded paper and fans' undying love for the team and their accomplishment poured upon the players…

The Zelig Cup

Frank Mazzullo, Bessie Mazzullo, Lisa O'Leary Mazzullo, Anthony Mazzullo, Sophia Kilbourne Mazzullo, Kathy Longo Mazzullo, John L. Mazzullo, Jake Mazzullo, James Patrick Mazzullo, Katherine Rose Mazzullo, Rose Fava, Joann Fava, Annette Fava, Anthony Fava, Tom Davis, Mike Montouri, Alan Cseh, Andy Edleman, Danny Phelan, Bob Fischetti, Ken Mahon, Mike Prezioso, Gary Kholhepp, Joe Imbo, Bob Hutchinson, Joe Devito, Steve Miata, Chris King, Phil Boyle, Mike Volgende, Mike O'Neill, Kevin O'Neill, Mike Lee, Andy Derosa, Sean Farrell, Jeff Ryan, Jeff Vanderbeek, Mark Landis, Mark Abrahamson, George Yorsack, Briank Linketter, Carol Linketter, Mike Lombardo

ABOUT THE AUTHOR

An aspiring writer in Wall Street, John Mazzullo has worked as a bond trader and investment manager for the MetLife Insurance Company for thirty-five years. However, this story has lived inside him since 1994. The proud, rookie author shares life with his wife, Kathy, and resides in pastoral Long Valley, New Jersey. The Mazzullo dynasty includes four remarkably adult children: John, Jake, James, and Katherine.